FAITHFUL AND TRUE

JOHN THOMSON

ISBN-10:1519459661
ISBN-13:978-1519459664

DEDICATION

To my Gashead family - thank you for this incredible new experience. The words within these pages are dedicated to Helen, Carole, Anthony, Gord, Beth, Meg, Jake, Claire, Simon, Dan, Carol, John, Mark, Chris, Stinky Bob, Mr Bear and Bella. And Big Bliss. UTG RTID

CONTENTS

Acknowledgments   i

1   Big Bliss   Pg 3

2   Madhouse   Pg 15

3   One Big Family   Pg 22

4   Pain   Pg 32

5   True Passion   Pg 35

6   Going Down   Pg 45

7   Fear the Beard   Pg 60

8   Trust   Pg 76

9   Awakened   Pg 82

10   Going Up   Pg 92

11   It's In The Cup   Pg 105

12   The Fortress   Pg 112

13   Memories of May   Pg 115

14   Gashead   Pg 126

ACKNOWLEDGMENTS

I'd like to thank Dover Athletic for their late equalizer against us at the Crabble Athletic Ground on the 18th of April 2015. If it hadn't been for that goal - I'd never awakened to something very special.

1 BIG BLISS

"We're onto the pitch. We're onto the pitch. If Blisset scores - we're onto the pitch!"

The chant from the Blackthorn End swirled and echoed around the ground and beyond as it drifted and disappeared into the streets and alleyways which meander and surround and embrace the Memorial Stadium - the home of Bristol Rovers Football Club. And it was within this hallowed place that seven thousand home supporters had their anguish turn to songful joy to revel in celebration whilst witnessing something which hadn't been witnessed at the Mem for a very long time - three points at home.

"We're onto the pitch. We're onto the pitch. If Blissett scores - we're onto the pitch!"

The vocal crescendo in song from the terraces was by no means an affirmation of the player's goal scoring prowess and had absolutely nothing to do with him having contributed in any way towards the reason why the Blue Army were on the verge of some kind mass elation which, if it was to continue, would surely see more than a few supporters discharging bodily fluids. No. I'm not referring to that. I'm referring to people who pee themselves when they're really happy or really excited. It happens. I know it happens because it happens to my partner when we go to music gigs. First we queue for hours. Then we push our way through the throng to get as close to the stage as is physically possible without actually being employed by the people who hand out plastic cups of water. Then we wait for another few hours until the curtain goes up on the main act as the first guitar chord is struck and thousands of fans scream and shout and start jumping up and down - including Helen who then pees herself. But that's another story for another book.

So it does happen. And it was on a cold Saturday in November that I genuinely thought the Blue Army was about to be soaked in a yellow flood of happiness as Nathan Blissett came on as a substitute with five minutes of the game still to be played. To be honest, it was more relief than excitement. Not relief that Big Bliss was on the pitch - because that's never a relief - but more the fact we'd pretty much won the match and our sub isn't allowed to go anywhere near our goalkeeper.

So we were happy. We were really happy. We'd had a relatively successful start to our new season after returning to the Football League (more of that in the pages that follow) and we were unstoppable away from home. It was almost as if our lads were scoring for fun whenever they found themselves on the road and away from the delights of the West Country. But our performances at home had been hexed and it had nothing to do with witchcraft. Visiting sides were aware and they took full advantage. These games had become dire and soul destroying to witness for Rovers supporters and we knew full well that we were sitting precariously in mid-table purely on away merit alone. But the table was turning on this chilly November afternoon - courtesy of two Matty Taylor strikes. Funny thing is, Taylor's no stranger to turning tables to try and find hidden silverware to get 'friendly' with (more of that too in the pages that follow).

"We're onto the pitch. We're onto the pitch. If Blissett scores - we're onto the pitch!"

Those words in song were raised all over the ground and they mixed with the rain before falling on the visiting Carlisle supporters who stood in the unsheltered away end. They looked miserable, cold and soaked. We were joyous and wet because we were about to win at home and it didn't matter that *Big Bliss* was on the park. Time had almost run out for him to not score again - hence the song - and seven thousand *Gasheads* braced themselves for the pitch invasion that would never happen.

Taylor's two goals had put us at ease. But the uneasy atmosphere before the start of the match had also been bolstered by a universal determination within the ground to get right behind the squad and give it all in our support of the team. And that resolve had come in the sound of song.

There had been such a negative social media build up to the match and the usual suspects were airing their discontent on the platforms of forums and websites affiliated with the club.

The mood was not good and the sky above the Mem on that match day was a mirror image of the atmosphere building in and around the stadium on Filton Avenue. I could understand why and I'm sure many others could too. It comes with the game. When passions run high it's bound to unleash fear and terror at some point. It's the realisation hitting home that home isn't where the heart should be and it has to be resuscitated quickly - because failure to get it pumping again could see another kind of horror emerge in the shape of a return to the place where the monsters live. We were in that darkness last season and we definitely don't want to go back there. We don't belong there. We're too good looking.

So cue the light in the sound of song. And nobody does it better than the thousand plus voices in the Blackthorn End. It was as if everyone had decided before the game that a mass aria - sung from Bristol bloodlines which pre-date the Roman conquest - would deafen the critics no matter the outcome of the game. And it worked. The cold terrace steps vibrated to the sound of passion and defiance and a new belief - bellowed in song with humour - was born.

I'd like to think I'm fairly quick off the mark. But I'm sure Helen would disagree - again. In saying that, she's never complained about me taking my time and she's always told me she much prefers it that way. But I'm digressing. You might find I do that a lot. So where were we? Oh yes, being quick off the mark. Let me put it this way - I can be sharp when I want to be and if I'm paying attention. But there are definitely a few gifted individuals within the Blackthorn throng who are nothing less than blessed when it comes to coming up with on-the-spot chant creation and the ability to get everyone else singing along in an instant. Now that must take some doing! It can't be easy? But it happens and it's a gift from the few to the many and it's incredible to experience. However, it may not be a positive experience for those on the receiving end – but that's not my concern. And anyway, it's highly likely the Carlisle fans had lost the ability to hear by that point. I've heard it's just one of the symptoms of hypothermia.

Deafening was the sound all around. The volume must have been turned up to eleven. And by this point, with all eyes on the referee's whistle, Blissett's song had become every other song following the arrival of a new composition. And it was this new entry which reinforced my own personal belief that the true and genuine football experience can only be found in the terraces of the lower football leagues. It can't be found anywhere else. It can't be found in the so-called exclusive, high end wining and dining areas which line the hospitality corridors of clubs which span the length and breadth of our footballing nation. Only questionable Man-of-the-Match accolades can be found in these places.

To find the true experience of the true football supporter requires a certain dedicated finesse to face and overcome and survive great personal harm in attempting to control scalding hot Bovril when your team scores and you find yourself juggling liquid lava as a half-eaten chicken tikka pie hits you square in the face. That's the true football experience. And it's from these lows that genius rises. From the concrete steps and steel crowd barriers – cold and hard – which supported generations of supporters before you and me, comes forth a funny defiance in the face of home result adversity. The words were true and they caught on immediately among the Blackthorn faithful. And thus, the still shivering visiting fans were subjected to the roar of *"We're winning at home. We're winning at home. How shit must you be? We're winning at home!"*

Whoever came up with that one deserves a free season ticket.

So there we are - a small group of *Gasheads* surrounded by thousands more – in full song in anticipation of the final whistle and also praying that Big Bliss doesn't score, because the last thing we need is for our six-foot-four front man to achieve the impossible at this specific moment in time by scoring a late third that could result in a pitch invasion which could see us fined or lose points at home –points which have eluded us months.

Can you imagine that? The long-suffering home win famine ends - only to be denied because of a goal from a player who can't score goals? It's just bonkers. And that's what was going through my mind as the seconds ticked away amid the sounds of victory above the hum of semi-silent and semi-conscious meditations taking place between some in the Blackthorn End and some almighty deity - praying for a striker to not score a goal. But that's what it's all about sometimes. Sometimes things aren't as clear cut when you're standing in the terracing,

"Please Thor - please don't let him hammer one past the keeper!"

To be fair - I like Big Bliss. I know I'm giving him a bit of a hard time right now, but he seems like a nice enough big bloke and I know in my heart that he's truly destined to do something magical on the pitch for Bristol Rovers at some point. It's just something I feel he'll do. Please don't ask me to explain why I feel this?

There's absolutely no evidence to suggest this prophecy will take place, based on his form since arriving from Kidderminster at the start of last season. He looks the part and I'm sure his height raises some concerns with the opposition when he lands in a game with seconds remaining. His stature must leave defenders convinced he's nothing less than an aerial combat ace with the ability to reach incoming high balls like a giraffe tonguing leaves. But I'm sure it doesn't take long for them to realise he's more like a very tall Bambi on ice.

Harsh? Maybe. But I'll also say this about him - he's about to awaken. There's something about him. You can see he thinks a great game - but the thoughts don't reach his feet. And I can absolutely guarantee you that when his football brain connects with the rest of his body - he will ravage opposition and the beautiful game will be blessed with another star. And then we'll lose him the same way we lost Rickie Lambert to glory with Southampton, England. Liverpool and West Bromwich Albion.

Lambert. He scored fifty one goals for Bristol Rovers between 2006 and 2009. Then to Southampton where he became their top scorer with one hundred and seventeen goals during a reign which helped them rise from League One to Championship to Premier League football in 2012. Rickie Lambert – one of us. Talent nurtured amid the streets and alleyways which meander and embrace a passion and fight which is faithful and true at the Memorial Stadium. But watch out Rickie - Big Bliss is warming up!

So the seconds were ticking away and the Carlisle supporters

were getting wetter and it wasn't because they were happy. Big
Bliss did actually come close to connecting his head with the
ball - but to no avail and the eruption of noise was deafening as
the referee blew the final whistle and we clinched our first home
League win since thumping Barnet 3-1 on the 22 August 2015.

Thirteen weeks. Unlucky? Perhaps. Shit strikers? Not really.
They were scoring for fun when playing away. So why the awful
home form before clinching the Carlisle victory?

Well, I've put a lot of thought to this and I blame Forest Green
Rovers FC. We had to play them last season in the Conference
League following our relegation to non-league football.

FGR can be found anchored in Nailsworth within the rolling
hills of Gloucestershire. But it's a paradox. The natural beauty
of the setting is smashed by the ugly truth of the FGR players.
And when I say a truth that's ugly - that's exactly what I mean.

Helen and I went to watch Rovers play there last season and we
won't be returning in a hurry. The experience turned out to be a
bit of a mind-feck (not sure if that's supposed to be
hyphenated) when the teams came out at the start of the game.
It takes a lot to shock me and even more to leave my good lady
speechless. It takes something which transcends shock to
silence Helen. And what we were about to witness did just that.

So it was a clear spring evening as the almost-twinkle of stars
shone down on the rolling countryside as the almost forgotten
chill of winter was bidding the south west a fond farewell for
another year.

I remember thinking, *"They should shoot the next Lord of the Rings
here."*

And it was with that thought - still fresh in my mind – that I
saw the teams emerge from the tunnel and my jaw hit the floor.

Our lads looked great. They always do. Some might even say we've got the sexiest squad in England. And I'd agree. But that's only to be expected. We're, without doubt, the sexiest supporters in the whole of the United Kingdom - so it's only fitting that our squad maintains the standards we set in the terracing.

But the FGR squad looked as if it could easily cast as the Orc Army. And they played like it too. The only welcome relief from this particular visual horror was that the home side had left their clubs and spears in the dressing room - but the downside was we were sure they still had teeth (although we weren't entirely convinced by some of their players) and they looked hungry.

Our lads had to suffer ninety minutes of medieval warfare but we still managed a win. So it just goes to show that good looks matter.

So I'm convinced our slow start to a successful home run in the current season is a direct result of the psychological harm caused by an away ordeal with the Orc Army in Gloucestershire. Is there any logic to what I've just written? Probably not. But I know in my heart it's true. And I'm okay with that. Just as I'm happy to never visit the stadium in Nailsworth ever again – because we all had to also endure the added trauma of paying for a ticket to watch football in a vegetarian venue. Yes, you heard me correctly. Forest Green Rovers doesn't allow meat to be consumed at the stadium. No munching on flesh. So yet another paradox, considering their first team looks capable of eating their ball boys.

So it's taking a bit of time to settle into the League again. Sure, we could do with more money to invest in new players and the likes - but what team in any league doesn't desire that? Exactly.

But more cash isn't going to bring heart and fight to our club. We don't need that. We've already got that and we've also got something more valuable than cash. We have a unique relationship with our players and our gaffer and it's because we're not bankrolled by a millionaire that we have this unique relationship. And it's so simple.

We have a real connection with the players. They have an affinity with us. There's no multi-million pound barrier between us and them and them and us. We can talk to them before the match and they can do the same with us. And because of this - we know that each and every one of our lads and our gaffer approaches each game with one single purpose in mind – to give all and play for the jersey.

The blue and white quarters of the relegated Blue Army marched the length and breadth of country last season in droves of thousands. We broke attendance records at nearly all of the away grounds we visited and I'm quietly confident we made many mobile burger van owners very wealthy indeed. And it was during that incredible football journey, to claw our way back to the Football League, that I fell in love with this club.

It's not just about the game. For me, it's about something so much more. It's about something football supporters from the lower leagues will understand. It's about supporting a team whose pitch you could hit if you walked out of your front door and lobbed a stone.

It's about the stone hitting someone you know in the clubhouse because everyone knows everyone else because you all live in the same town or city and most of you were likely born in the same town or city. It's a community supporting a football team which represents the history of everyone in the community.

It's about the colours you wear and share with folk who you work alongside and live alongside. And these colours adorned stand shoulder to shoulder in their thousands on concrete steps and beneath rusting corrugated roofing in a display of unity and community which sparked to life all those years ago and remains to this very day. It's a day which is all days with at least one single thought solely dedicated to the game you've just seen and the match that awaits. And it's these thoughts which bridge your waking existence between away journeys and home encounters as post-match analysis ebbs away to the emergence of your own team selection for the next game - which the club's gaffer always seems to get not quite right.

It's about previewing the game on matchday over a full English with fellow *Gashead* friends in Wetherspoons in Kingswood - a Bristol suburb and BRFC stronghold - as you inadvertently position your hash browns, sausages and bacon in a four-four-two formation whilst pondering whether it's wrong to have the occasional (occasional) fantasy of what it would be like to share a special encounter with Darrell Clarke - the young gaffer who openly wept on the day we were relegated to the Conference League and then single-handedly inspired his team and thousands of us to promotion again after ONE season with a finale ending at Wembley.

It's a fantasy which is definitely occasional but it's a fantasy which is perfectly justified.

It's about more than money. It's about a community with a history. It's about highs and lows and aspirations swathed in a sea of blue and white - which roars in sound as our lads emerge from the tunnel and we stand by them through thick and thin - because that's what we do for one another. We stand close at the beginning and we stay 'til the end. We never walk away. Generations of history won't allow us. And so we never will.

We're Bristol Rovers. *The Gas. The Pirates* - the name we embrace courtesy of our city's proud maritime history.

Gashead. That's what they called us all those years ago in an attempt to belittle us. They meant it to be derogatory. But as always - they got it wrong.

Gashead. The name was born from the location of where our true home used to stand - Eastville Stadium. Nearby was a gasworks. And so the smell from the works would occasionally waft across the ground. So our rivals - Bristol City - gave us the name *Gasheads*. And it stuck. It stuck because we embraced the name since it has an invisible potency to it. And that sits with us - much to the disappointment of 'them down the road'. When it comes to being a football supporter in Bristol you're either blessed or burdened. Bristol Rovers or Bristol City. I'm one of the lucky ones. I'm blessed!

So how did I become blessed as a *Gashead* when I'm not even from Bristol? I'm from Glasgow. How is that possible? Well it happened to me like it happens to so many others. And the strange thing is it was a moment of misery during an away match in Dover which sparked a truth within me - a truth which awakened a realisation that I'd become part of something so very special.

My name is John Thomson. I was born in Scotland and I'm a former Scottish Television journalist, football producer and director.

Bristol is now my home. It has been for the past five years and I'll explain why later. But it was to the warm and welcoming embrace of this city that I found a new life after years of hurt. And it was within this warm and welcoming embrace that I found a new love in my life. Helen. She gave me a chance when no others would. And the gift of her was to gift to me another love. Another passion. Another family amid the blue and white quarters of the Blue Army. And it's with a smile that I say I'm one of them. I'm not alone anymore. And it's with a bigger smile that I say I'm a *Gashead*. And that's something to be proud of...

Irene, good night Irene,

Irene goodnight.

Goodnight Irene, goodnight Irene,
I'll see you in my dreams.

2 MADHOUSE

I'm sitting in our living room right now as I write these words.

It's a beautiful clear and crisp November morning outside and it's nice and snug inside. A Christmas candle burns on the mantelpiece, the blinds are down and the only light in the room is courtesy of a single lamp. Fuck me, I'm good. How's that for ambience?

I feel it's important to note at this point that I'll do my best to refrain from indulging in expletives. I'll do my very best. But when it comes to swearing - it tends to be a genetic thing. I'm from Glasgow and it comes with the territory. However, I'm sure some of you reading right now may be averse to this kind of written word. So I'll be scripting bad words in a slightly different way, so as not to offend any sensitive types among you. From now on, fuck will be feck. You okay with that? I hope so, because I have no fecking way of knowing if you are or not. But let's give it a go anyway.

But I do have to say that I'll be using the 'C' word every now and again. I know it's a bad one and it's the one word which induces revulsion with most civilised types. And you've just bought this book - so that means you're probably civilised too? I'm sure you are. I'm sure you're nodding and smiling right now. But don't worry – I'll do my very best to limit the number of times I use the 'C' word. I know how upsetting it can be - especially for vulnerable people and young children. But I'm afraid there's no alternative. I will be mentioning Bristol City FC periodically throughout this book. If I leave out the 'City' – it just reads Bristol. And that's incorrect. Some television football pundits should take note of this too.

I did phone BCFC earlier today and I asked them if they'd mind changing their name to Bristol United? I told them I didn't want to use the 'C' word in my new book. But they told me to feck off.

So, as I was saying – there's a lovely ambience in the room this morning as I'm writing these words for you. What's not quite ambient is the cat doing his best to rub his arse in my face. And what makes matters worse - he's a Preston North End fan. I kid you not.

Stinky Bob is pure white - hence his love for the Lilywhites. We took him from someone we knew because they weren't looking after him properly. His hind legs don't work and he's deaf. We also reckon he's a bit 'slow'. That's also contributing towards his affinity to the lads from Deepdale. And he's the current culprit who's trying his best to make me kiss his little ring.

The other one is called Mr. Bear and he used to be a Liverpool supporter. Well, to be honest, he was really just a Beatles fan who fell in love with Suarez. It was the biting 'thing' which he idolised. Mr. Bear is a natural born killer. There isn't anything smaller than a small dog left alive on our street – courtesy of our fat psycho murdering pet. He was gutted (now he knows what it feels like) when Suarez left Anfield. He's still a Beatles fan but he now supports Stoke City. No one is brave enough to ask why? It's best to just leave him alone with his Soccer Saturday Super Six.

Our house is a busy house and our pets are bonkers - so they're not out of place in our residence in Hanham.

We're all into sport in our house and football is generally on the telly, all of the time, in some shape or form. And the teams being supported vary, with Bristol Rovers, Arsenal and Spurs featuring most of the time on our flat screen. But there is another side which features in our house and I'm extremely wary of mentioning we have 'one of them' in our home.

It staggers me because he's a genuinely nice lad and I love him like a son. He's well-mannered and he's even toilet trained. He's got a good job and he works really hard. He's even good looking! It just doesn't make sense to me how he can support *'them down the road'*.

I've seen *'them down the road'*. I saw them at close quarters in 2013. We were drawn away against Bristol City in a cup tie and there was nothing which could've prepared me for what I was to witness.

Now I'm no stranger to the love not shared at Derby matches. I'm from Glasgow and I'm a veteran of many Old Firm clashes between Celtic and Rangers - courtesy of the work I used to do up there. In my experience of these games - it was as if the football was incidental during the ninety minutes of hate. Unbelievable. And yet I'd recommend one of these matches to any football supporter to witness at least once in a lifetime.

So I thought I'd seen it all. And when we were drawn away against City - I found myself being tentatively informed that it might be wise to not buy a ticket for the match because there would definitely be trouble.

My riposte to this (seasoned by years of witnessing a stormy sea of green and white and blue try to smash the shit out of one another) was a simple, yet loud guffaw to the skies as I thought, "I've survived the fiercest Derby clash the world has ever known. This is going to be child's play!"

But I was wrong. We did go to the game and it was unlike anything I'd ever seen before. It wasn't child's play at all. But a lot of the City fans did look and behave like Chucky. I actually saw one of the home supporters meander through the security cordon of yellow high visibility jackets and up to the corner of the pitch as the game kicked off. He grabbed the corner flag and decided it would make a great javelin. To be honest - it was a disturbingly creative attempt and the bloke deserves top marks for the horrific blend of ingenuity and stupidity. And so with a dull 'the lights are on but no one is home' glaze over his eyes - he tried to spear us. Fortunately no one was hurt. And now we all know he'll never make the cast to the sequel of 300.

But the rest of us have to and a lot happened that night. It was definitely an experience to remember and we did ourselves proud. We lost 2-1 but we sang our hearts out and they'll never be able to take that away from us. The game ended and the City supporters invaded the pitch in an attempt to antagonise us away from our end for a confrontation on the turf. It didn't happen.

They did their best to get a reaction. But it didn't happen. What did happen was the Blue Army standing its ground and singing Goodnight Irene. It's been our anthem since 1950 when it was sung by Bristol Rovers supporters to Plymouth Argyle fans as they were leaving our ground before the final whistle because we were winning. But we don't just sing it when we're winning.

We sang it loud as the City fans amassed on the pitch. Our reply to their baying for blue blood was to fill the murky air around Ashton Gate with the sweet sound of *"Irene Goodnight Irene. Irene goodnight. Goodnight Irene, goodnight Irene, I'll see you in my dreams"*

I think this just infuriated the home supporters. They were jumping up and down on their own pitch with no one to fight and they were surrounded by police and mounted officers. And while all of this was going on - the television commentary team who'd covered the game live were saying, *"The Bristol Rovers fans are doing their club proud. They're just standing and singing their hearts out. A fine example to football supporters!"*

This must have enraged the winning side's fans even more. They were up for causing trouble but trouble wasn't interested. So they did what any civilised person would do - they started punching police horses!

It was highly entertaining and great value for money. The horses didn't flinch. It was a bit like watching a deranged and extremely drunk and dribbling minion having a go at a woolly mammoth. The outcome was predictable. My money was on the contender with teeth. And I won a fiver in five minutes when the minion was hit over the head with a baton and dragged away in handcuffs.

We may have lost - but we did ourselves proud in defeat and the post- match show on the pitch was an unexpected encore which definitely merited an additional few quid on the ticket price.

It was a Derby night to remember as we made our way to the BRFC supporters buses. There was also a bit of mayhem outside the stadium - but nothing a few toothy ponies hell bent on revenge couldn't sort out. Have you ever been bitten by a horse? I have. It hurts. So I'm sure a lot of GP surgeries in the Bedminster area of Bristol were inundated with requests for horse bite soothing creams the following morning.

The night was almost over and the moon shone high above. We

just had to stay low to avoid the airborne missiles of home supporters' beer bottles filled with pee. I'll give them their due - they know how to keep their press office busy. And as for the pee in bottles? I sincerely hope they filled them themselves? The uncomfortable alternative is they're buying them full from somewhere on their side of the river.

So I remain staggered that one of 'them' is in our house. But as I've said - he's a good lad and we love him to bits. It's very true what they say - you can pick your friends but you can't pick your family. I won't tell you his name. I wouldn't do that to him. He'll want to stay well away from the words within these pages. And that's okay. I try not to upset his routine. So it's best he doesn't know I'm writing about him. It's taken a long time to finally get him settled. Twenty three years. But if he does find out and he does get upset - I know what to do. I just plonk him down in front of the telly - give him a bowl of spaghetti hoops with some toast soldiers and press play on his SpongeBob DVD. It works every time.

The rest of us are sane - but only to others who share our own particular kind of insanity. But on a serious note – we do have a lovely family and I'm a very lucky man to have them all in my life. And to be honest, if it wasn't for Helen - I wouldn't be a *Gashead*.

Two sides of the Bristol Derby living together and represented under one roof. It may sound odd but it's hardly unique and we all have a great time together, winding one another up when results favour one side over the other.

This season is proving the perfect source for mischievous speculation on whether there's a real possibility that Bristol could see league derbies next season, considering the current positions of both sides in their respective league tables. The banter's always on form and that's the way it should be.

But in my short time as a *Gashead*, I've often wondered why they despise us so much? They're currently bobbing along in the Championship, but they're forever more concerned about what we're up to, up our way? It seems incessant and some might say we're their obsession. But the 'why' eludes me.

Our rivals have always referred to us as *Tinpot* or *Ragbag*. Fair enough - we've never enjoyed the indulgences which they've enjoyed. But as I've already mentioned – it's not just about money and big signings. It's about history and community and solidarity. We have all three and we stay 'til the end. We don't take flight when we're losing – a common occurrence in the land of the Robin. We stay 'til the end. We may not always applaud the end – but we do stay. That says something about our fans. Money can't buy that. That's priceless.

Carl Jung - the eminent Swiss psychiatrist and psychotherapist – said, *"Everything that irritates us about others can lead us to an understanding of ourselves."*

Jung was a genius and is universally regarded as the father of head medicine. So I've reached two conclusions. The first is they hate us because they see a success in us which can't be purchased and it's the kind of 'success' they'll probably never have. And my second conclusion is they're really unhappy because our turf resides on top of a hill and we've got lovely views in the summer, whereas they live down by the smelly river – hence the saying, *'them down the road'*.

Property wars are a bitch!

3 ONE BIG FAMILY

It's like a family. That's the best way to describe it. And I think it's the only way to describe it.

Standing together in the Blackthorn End through thick and thin in highs and lows with joy and pain in sleet and snow and rain and sun.

Weathered by elation or soul-destroying hurt - the results which befall each and every game always have the same effect. We keep coming back to the Memorial Stadium.

The spot to where we always return is a very special place within a very special place. The North Stand is also known as the Blackthorn End and that's where all the serious *Gasheads* can be found. No seats are required for this lot and the concrete steps beneath the corrugated iron roof can accommodate nearly four thousand of us when the fixture commands it. And I've seen it almost this full on a few occasions.

The noise can be deafening as West Country faithful from far and wide amass on one spot in the suburb of Horfield to get right behind a team which saw its beginnings born in 1883 as Black Arabs FC. And it's more than likely that many of the present voices in song hail directly from the first supporters to watch the Arabs play in another part of our city one hundred and thirty two years ago.

The Memorial Stadium - affectionately known as *The Mem* - has only been our home since 1996. The decade preceding was spent at Twerton Park in Bath where we ground shared with Bath City and was known by the *Gasheads* as *Trumpton*. And before this time was a place regarded as our spiritual home - Eastville Stadium.

Eastville was our home from 1897 to 1986. We were once known as Eastville Rovers and even Bristol Eastville Rovers before changing our name to Bristol Rovers in 1899.

Eastville and Twerton still resonate within the fondly shared memories among the *Gashead* faithful in the clubhouse before kick-off, as a few cheeky pints are enjoyed among friends to the fond memories of glory days of old when Bristol Rovers was no stranger to success at the highest level and silencing our arch rivals on the pitch was a regular occurrence.

I'm no club historian and I don't profess to be. I'm just a fan who's fallen in love with the club and I find my own kind of solace in writing words. The days of old in success for Bristol Rovers have been shared to me by the woman I love and the truest of friends I've made whilst standing in the Blackthorn End every other Saturday. And it's because of this welcome into the Blue Army that I'm writing this book. It's just my way of saying thank you.

Thank you for this incredible experience. Thank you for being part of something present and past which I never thought I'd have. It's a privilege to now be part of something which began all those years ago in a time and place unforgotten - unforgotten thanks to memories in stories which are sometimes shouted and sometimes whispered among the blue and white all around me.

I hear your history spoken true and it's almost as if I was there with you. And it feels as if I'm there with you in another time, in another space, because your memories are shared from your heart and it's within your heart that a passion born from fight and love and history resounds and I hear it and I feel it too. Echoes of Eastville twinned with times at Twerton. The glory days of Bristol Rovers. Never forgotten by all of us - should never be forgotten by those who aren't one of us.

There's one game which I wish I could've been at. Amid all the stories and memories of old - there's one that stands out to me and it's one that have some kind of connection with, even though I wasn't there.

The 2nd of May 1990.

I know Joe Jordan. I met Joe a few times during my time as a football producer with Scottish Television in Glasgow. And I can honestly say you won't meet a nicer bloke

I produced a programme called Scotsport for a number of years. It was Scotland's version of Match of the Day - and that meant there was a regular turnover of studio pundits depending on the featured match. This also applied to UEFA Champions League output and I was also responsible for producing and directing live highlights programming. So with the Old Firm featuring in the competition - Celtic and Rangers were up against Europe's best and for those games we'd call in the 'big guns' for live studio match coverage. And Joe Jordan was one of the 'big guns'.

I'm by no means saying we're best mates. We don't play golf together and he's stopped sending me Christmas cards. We worked together a few times and he's first-class - quite a quiet man but nothing less than a legend in my eyes.

I have so many fine memories of watching Jordan play for Manchester United when I was a wee boy. Hairy and toothless. That's Joe - not me! Incredible player. Lots of hair. No teeth. So it was a humbling experience to actually meet him and work with him - and others who I'd idolised as a boy.

I probably won't go into too much detail about my twelve years with Scottish Television. I don't want the book to focus too much on that. But there are many connections between my work back then and my passion for BRFC in the here and now.

I started working as a runner with STV in 1994. I was literally in the right place at the right time when the opportunity arose and I found myself being offered unpaid work with the broadcaster. And it was to be the beginning of a whole new and incredible life experience for me.

I'll always feel privileged to have learned from and worked with the best in the world of television media. And it's courtesy of the skill set which I acquired during that time that I now find myself a freelance documentary filmmaker in the south west of England. And the reason why I'm here is something I'll touch on in a wee bit.

I worked my way up from unpaid runner to paid researcher to a contract as a journalist/reporter with the Scottish Television newsroom in 1996. And it was the following year that I was offered a job as an assistant producer in the sports department.

The sports department was a world within a world and I couldn't believe I was actually getting paid to produce football programming whilst working with players who were and are nothing less than icons to me growing up.

I remember one day at my desk when my phone rang and it was security informing me that Danny McGrain had arrived and was sitting in reception.

McGrain probably isn't well known south of Hadrian's Wall - but he was regarded as one of the best full-backs in the world in the seventies. A Celtic and Scotland legend - Danny was nothing less than a childhood hero to me.

McGrain had arrived to take part in the studio recording of a programme dedicated to Celtic FC. The producer of that programme was running around like a lunatic trying to get his production running order finalised - so he asked me if I wouldn't mind grabbing Danny from downstairs and taking him to the green room for a cuppa? I said no problem. And made my way across the office and headed for the lift.

It hit me when I was in the lift. I was about to meet Danny McGrain. Danny McGrain. Memories came flooding back of me watching McGrain in the blue of Scotland and the green and white hoops of Celtic. Danny McGrain. One of my childhood heroes. One of so many who used to leave me captivated and in awe as I sat cross-legged in front a television screen in the seventies and eighties. Danny McGrain.

The lift door opened and I walked into STV reception. I was a bumbling gibbering mess and I'd lost the power of speech as I stumbled towards him and offered my hand. And Danny was brilliant. He just smiled and said hello in a very unassuming way because he's a very unassuming man. He's also a lot shorter than I remembered him when I was a boy. He's shrunk from about seven feet to about five foot six. But he's still a giant to me.

He always will be and there are so many others like him who I've met and they're just like him. They were incredible in their own individual heydays and they're humbling to work with. There's no airs and graces with those generations of footballers. From my own personal experiences of producing programming with them - they all maintain a very down to earth and quite humble persona. I was lucky enough to meet a few of them from those eras and I was always left impressed. Danny McGrain, Kenny Dalglish, Alan Rough, Graeme Souness, Derek Johnstone, Mark Hately, Alan McInally and Alex McLeish. And Joe Jordan.

I met another legend during my time with Scottish Television. A legend from a more recent era and it wasn't the kind of meeting you might associate with this former player. I'll never forget the goal he scored against us during Euro '96 at Wembley. I've never seen anything like it since and I'm not sure if I ever will. You know the saying, "Can you remember where you were when Elvis died?" Well, I can clearly recall where I was when this footballing great graced the world with perfection and put the goal of all goals past his Rangers team mate, Andy Goram.

I was in a pub in Glasgow on that beautiful sunny day in June. Trader Joes was the STV local and it was always filled with us lot. The pub was rammed when that goal was scored and hundreds of jaws hit the floor - including my own. But what I remember most about the seconds that followed was the stunned acceptance of what we'd just witnessed. It couldn't be faulted. You can't fault genius. So no one said anything and we all just ordered another drink – in silence.

I have a lot of respect for that man. But I'll tell you about that meeting in a more appropriate part of the book later on.

Joe Jordan. The second day of May 1990.

I wasn't at Twerton Park on that glorious day when ten thousand supporters packed the Bath ground. But I have heard about it from Helen. She was there. And I wish I had been too.

I've watched the highlights so many times and I never tire of seeing Big Devon White and Ian Holloway clinch the three goals to secure what was and arguably remains our greatest ever win over 'them down the road' to ensure the Third Division title. But what shocked me and still shocks me is how Joe Jordan was shouted at and spat upon by his so-called supporters - while other City fans thought it was a good idea to destroy advertising boards and throw them onto the pitch.

I really feel for Jordan every time I watch that archive footage. No manager deserves that from opposition supporters, let alone their own. It must have been so embarrassing for him and Bristol City. But maybe there was a different culture back then? Maybe supporters behave better now? Well, I can only go by what I've witnessed in the present day. And what I've seen is one team in Bristol standing and singing after losing and one team in Bristol running riot and punching police horses on their own pitch after winning. I think I've just answered my own question.

Now don't get me wrong. I'm not naive. Intense rivalry between two clubs in the same city is what makes Derby matches a bit special. I love them. I don't think football would be the same without these kind of unique rivalries. It's the best ninety minutes around - unless you're a bit flush with a few readies in Soho after watching Arsenal versus Spurs. But come on - there's no need to attack Trigger!

Some say it's a tribal thing? In Glasgow it's a sectarian thing. Sometimes it's a political thing. And sometimes it's just a jealous thing.

So they envy our Blackthorn End and it's in this hallowed place where source or sources of these former days of glory come in many shapes and forms. They're mostly the people who I stand with at home games and the wealth of knowledge and personal experiences among our friends in the stand is impressive to say the least.

First and foremost is my partner Helen. As I've already said, she was the one who took me to my first match at the Mem in 2013. We'd only been together for six months and it felt really good for me to be watching football again. I'd stopped watching the game for a number of years after leaving Scottish Television in 2006 - and so it was time to return to the terracing to watch the game which had played such a massive part of my life in Glasgow.

To be honest, I was still a Celtic supporter at the time. But that was to change during a Bristol Rovers Conference League away match in Dover this year. But there's a lot to share before I share about that day.

So Helen and I started going to matches together and it was at the Memorial Stadium where I was introduced to Claire and Simon and so many other BRFC supporters. And it just felt right for me and I was made to feel very welcome and always have been by everyone at the club - even though I'm not from this part of the country.

Helen is Bristol through and through. And if having a lush bottom is a prerequisite to being Bristolian - then Helen is Bristol through and through and through.

Now, 'lush' is a word widely used in Bristol. It means nice. And it forms a very important part of communication in the West Country - including the addition of the word 'mind' to the end of every sentence.

An example of this would be, instead of saying, *"We need to go to town to buy a nice sofa"* you'd say, *"We need to go to town to buy a lush sofa, mind."* I just thought I'd clear that up in the event of you thinking I'd lost my command of English grammar. It's just that it's starting to rub off on me and I'm finding more and more that I'm wandering around sounding like a pirate these days. So don't worry. No keel hauling in the pages that come. Well, I hope not - because I haven't seen anyone keel hauled at the

Mem yet. But it's still early days and if this current lack of form at home continues - it's more than likely that some poor sod could end up suffering that particular fate. But enough of Big Bliss!

There are many other Bristolian-isms. I may use them - I may not. They include *proper, gert* and *me babber*. The first two are used instead of 'really' and the third means 'my love'. So if you can now decipher this, then you're ready to move to the west country, *'Helen is me babber and she has a proper gert lush arse'*.

Got it? Good. Moving swiftly on…

So we met for a cuppa in the suburb of Kingswood in the autumn of 2012 and I liked her from the start. She did tell me later that she didn't think I was her type when she first saw me. And to be fair - Adonis is never really a label I've ever been labelled with. But she did also tell me later that she liked me too, after about ten minutes of chatting over our cappuccinos. So our opening encounter together ended a one-one draw.

So we decided to meet again and then we fell in love. We're still together and she's been a Bristol Rovers supporter most of her life.

Helens passion for the club was born from her stepdad - Gordon. Gord, as he was known, was a lovely and gentle man who is no longer with us. But it was Gord who took Helen to her first-ever match at Twerton Park - and that's where her love affair with the blue and white quarters began. And it's where her fondest memories of being a *Gashead* remain.

I wish I could've met Gord. He was married to Helen's mum - Carole - and I believe he was a very special and kind man. And I can see why Carole and Gord ended up together - because Carole is a lovely woman and she's also a passionate Rovers fan. If Gord hadn't been around, then Helen probably wouldn't have gone to her first match at Twerton all those years ago. And if she hadn't gone – then she wouldn't have fallen head-over-heels with the Rovers and wouldn't have taken me to my own first game in 2013.

And I now can't imagine what it would be like to not be part of the BRFC family. It's unique.

There are many who I've dedicated this book to. So many new faces in my life now and I feel blessed to be part of this Blue Army. It may sound odd – but that's just how I feel. I can be a soppy sod at times – just like I'm being now. But this club's supporters have made a massive impression on me and their welcome to me is something I can't really describe in words. But I'm going to have to try - because I'm writing a fecking book about it!

And so I'm writing these words and it's just a few hours before we kick-off against Stevenage at the Mem tonight. So our Gas Gang will once again gather beneath the corrugated iron roof of the Blackthorn End and the members are Claire, Simon, Carol, Mark, John, Sam, Chris, Chris' dad and Chris' dad's brother. Dan used to be a gang member. Dan belongs to Claire and Simon. Well, he doesn't belong to them. He's their son. But he invested in a more expensive season ticket and he now has a seat in the east stand. And every now and again he blesses us with a wave and a smile from high yonder. We smile and wave back. And it's just as well he can't hear us.

So I hope we'll be doing more than smiling and waving at Dan tonight. I really hope we all enjoy another much needed home win. We're just four points off a play-offs position in the league and three points tonight would be nothing less than gert lush. I'll see you later. Up the Gas!

4 PAIN

Bristol Rovers v Stevenage
Memorial Stadium, Tuesday 24th November 2015

And so the final whistle blows and you stand alone with those who remain and gaze into the floodlit night sky and wonder what the hell just happened and what the hell you've just witnessed during the ninety minutes that have just come and gone.

You stand alone with others nearby who you know feel the same and watch your team in blue and white wander across the pitch beneath the artificial light as they raise their hands to applaud you for your support - so you pull your hands out of your pockets and return to them a half-hearted salute. And it's that half of heart that's causing the hurt within you as you step down on the concrete steps to get just that little bit closer to the pitch to applaud your manager who's walking off the pitch behind the players and applauds the Blackthorn End where you return his gaze.

You wait until he disappears down the tunnel and then you turn and climb the cold stairs of the terrace as you feel a mixture of anger and disappointment and confusion as yet again you've watched the team you love crash 2-1 in yet another home defeat and the thought you'd hoped and prayed you'd ever think of again makes an unwelcome appearance in your mind as you remember non-league as you depart the Memorial Stadium beneath the full moon of night and pass through the gates and turn left onto Filton Avenue.

The black of night is bombarded with headlights and streetlights as you turn onto Gloucester Road and it's almost as if you wish you could disappear into the darkness because it feels as if every passenger in every car and every bus that races by knows what's just happened and you don't want them to know.

So you walk a bit faster and then turn left again into Strathmore Road and there's a small sense of relief because it's quiet and darker and offers a safer place to hide as your pace slows because there are no more watchful eyes from the bright light traffic spotlighting your hurt.

From Strathmore to Downend to Springfield Road. You're moving further and further away from the place that's filled you with elation in times and games gone by and your mind struggles to remember why you do what you do to end up feeling the way you do as you approach your car and fall in.

You turn on the radio despite what you've just seen and despite how you feel and listen to the match reaction on BBC Radio Bristol and it's nothing less than a miracle that your brain can actually function to allow you to navigate a one tonne vehicle onto Muller Road towards home and at the same time analyse the post- match analysis which is smothering the airways with, *"The keeper has to go!"* to *"We need a striker"* to *"I think the chicken tikka pie has given me worms!"*

You've heard it all before (well, maybe not the worms thing but you've always denied yourself the delights of a chicken tikka pastie because it looks nothing less than foul) and you know it isn't going to change because it's unlikely there's a pot full of cash to buy players and it's always been that way and the gaffer is doing the best he can with what he has available and he should've received a knighthood after last season.

You're nearly home and you hear the radio presenter hand over to the reporter at the stadium you're moving quickly away from and he introduces your manager for his own views of the game. He starts to talk and he's making sense because it is a tough league and there are bound to be lows and we have to accept that we're going to get the occasional kick in the teeth. And with that you realise he's absolutely spot on and it's only one game and we've been there before and we fought our way back whilst he was at the helm.

And so the minutes pass and eventually you're home and you still feel gutted and you're still feeling confused and hurt, but you know you have faith in your manager and your team because it's not just any manager and team - it's Bristol Rovers FC.

The pain and the anger begin to subside and it's with the half heart you had at the end of the game which commanded you to applaud your team and manager that you begin to look forward to Saturday and your trip to Exeter with the woman you love and two of your dearest friends who are also Gasheads. And so it begins again. Onto the next match. Into hope that we can get a much needed three points. But one point would do.

And that's the way it is. That's the game. Welcome to your life as a football supporter. Great when you're celebrating. Shit when you're not. And I wouldn't have it any other way.

5 TRUE PASSION

"I reckon the ball was travelling at 400mph and I bet it burned the keeper's eyebrows off!"

Ian Holloway was referring to a QPR goal at Crewe. That was his post-match reaction. But I'm quietly convinced he was somehow also referring to our keeper Lee Nicholls and that second Stevenage strike from last night. It's almost as if Ollie isn't just a philosopher with a unique and rare insight into all that takes place on and off the pitch - but it's highly likely he's some kind of prophet too. Is it actually possible that Holloway can jump into space and time to see what many cannot and will not ever see? My answer is yes. I believe he's a very special and gifted man whose own deep and personal and profound awakening of soul and spirit was lifted and elevated by the footballing Gods after he netted that penalty at Twerton on that second day in May in 1990. And what was to follow was nothing less than a man being reborn to share divine messages to the world within words of wisdom for the grace of the beautiful game.

"I reckon the ball was travelling at 400mph and I bet it burned the keeper's eyebrows off!"

He saw it coming. He definitely saw it coming. Ollie's visionary foresight saw it coming - but that didn't help Nicholls. Our keeper had no chance against Chris Whelpdale's rocket from 20 yards. But I'm sure he did see the almost-full-moon and the ball at the same time in a split second as both spheres became one circle - as celestial delight mixed with high speed synthetic horror. He didn't stand a chance. Not even if he had Kenny Everett's hands. And it's not the first time. Just three days earlier saw our number thirty one fall foul of yet another missile attack - courtesy of Rhys Murphy's 25 yarder when we were away to Crawley. Nicholls must be thinking he's done something to upset NATO.

I sincerely hope this isn't true. I like Nicholls. I know there's currently speculation he may be leaving before the end of the year. I hope not. I know he's been caught out a few times since arriving at *The Mem* and now he may be for the off - back to Wigan Athletic - but I think that would be a bit unfair. He's still finding his feet and we need to give him some time - because he's still trying to find his hands and he can't find his feet without his hands.

And as for sending him back to Wigan? Why would you want to do that to him? Wigan? He only managed to escape in September after he refused to take part in their well-known and much-loved Sunday evening pursuit of hunting witches. Why on earth would you want to send anyone back to that? Especially now, when he's just getting used to running water, mobile phones and when he no longer needs stabilisers on Ellis Harrison's exercise bike! Give him a chance

So we need to be patient with him. It can't be easy being a goalie. To be honest - I think you have to be a bit *'not quite right upstairs'* to want to put yourself in that kind of position. I mean, let's be honest - who in their right mind would want to face ten players whose only intense desire is to humiliate you by putting the ball past you as you stand with your back to hundreds or even thousands of opposition supporters baying for your blood within a chorus of *"You're shit"* whilst doing their very best to reach out to you with a chicken tikka pie which tends to not be aerodynamic?

Indeed. Not me either. And then you add the added misery of having certain parts of your facial hair removed by a 400mph rocket disguised as a ball? No thanks. I'd much rather don my blue and white quarters and run around outside Ashton Gate on a match day - handing out bars of soap whilst whistling the song which is much-loved down Bedminster way - *'Gypsies, Tramps and Thieves'*.

It can't be easy standing in goals. And I sincerely hope NATO aren't after him. But if they are, then at least he's half way there in attaining a new disguise. With no eyebrows, all he now has to do is remove the rest of the hair from his head and I'm sure the special forces with orders to eliminate him will find it harder to succeed in their mission. But that's only as long as NATO aren't also looking for Jaap Stam!

So the Oracle that is Ollie strikes true yet again. A Bristol Rovers legend and it's great to see and hear him on the telly these days. I've never met him. But Helen has. He's one of her all-time BRFC heroes and in her own words she says, *"He's such a lovely, lovely man!"*

I love hearing Helen share about her highs and lows as a *Gashead*. I love hearing them because I can identify with her now. My own highs and lows are obviously from the here and now and from the past few seasons. But there's another connection between us now and it's very special to me.

Helen's reminiscing of Rovers' victories gone by are a joy for me hear. And because I'm now also passionate about the club - it's almost as if I'm with her in times past when she shares about them. I can see her drift away in her eyes when she remembers her BRFC anointing at Twerton Park and how she later worked in the hotdog stand at Eastville and served and laughed with fellow *Gasheads* before and during each match in a time and a place which will always be dear to those who were there. And I wish I'd been there too. But in many ways I am there and I'm there in those times when we visit Helen's mum - Carole - and they both start chatting about those days.

I really hope you're enjoying reading these words? As I've already mentioned - those Rovers days of old play no part in my own personal experience as a Gashead. I'm new to this family. But even though I wasn't there and even though I didn't stand with you at Twerton Park on that second day in May in 1990 - I feel as if I was. And I feel privileged to be part of Helen's and Carole's memories - as well as yours. I've met so many lovely and genuine people since I lost my mind and fell in love with this club. So many of you have welcomed me home - and it's really for all of you that I'm writing these words. You already know a wee bit about me. You know where I come from and you know what I used to do in Glasgow. So it wouldn't surprise me if any of you are wondering why Bristol Rovers?

Helen's family has obviously played a massive part in me falling for the blue and white quarters - but there's more.

I come from a family which is divided in its Old Firm allegiance. My dad grew up on the Catholic side of the sectarian divide and my mum grew up on the other. They met and fell in love and that was that. I don't think it went down too well with some people to begin with. It was the sixties. But it all worked out both families became very close and I have fond and warm memories of being a wee boy growing up in Clydebank - not far from Glasgow.

I think one of my earliest and dearest memories is getting a Scotland football strip for Christmas. I must have been about seven or eight. My wee brother received one from Santa too and I remember how we put on our navy jerseys with the Lion Rampant badges and kicked a ball about on a frozen and muddy park opposite our house on Jowitt Avenue.

It was 'jumpers for goalposts' time and we just ran around and around with the ball and my dad until it started to get dark and colder - to then be called inside to the warm by my mum. I remember it well. I remember the joy of wearing my strip and the feeling of cold air in my chest and the day drew in and what seemed like a frosty white mist falling gently down on the three of us. And then we went inside to the many colours glowing in and around the tree as they added their own rainbow of warmth to our home as Freddy Mercury and Queen sang Bohemian Rhapsody on Top of the Pops.

Happy days for a wee boy. Really happy days as I felt so proud to be wearing a jersey which Santa had also given players like Kenny Dalglish, Andy Gray, Danny McGrain and Joe Jordan. Football was and always has been part of me in some shape or form - but it never awakened a passion. That was to happen much later in my life.

That was to happen at Dover on the 18th of April 2015.

My dad played a massive part in introducing me to the game. I suppose most dads do. You'll still find him at his happiest when he's got his feet up in front of the telly - enjoying a cheeky tipple whilst watching a game on the telly. He used to be a really good player when he was younger. He played in a Scottish Junior Cup Final when he was only sixteen and I'm sure I've heard it mentioned that Celtic were looking at him around that time. He's a lovely man. Very quiet and unassuming. But he hasn't always been that way.

Jimmy Cairney is my dad's oldest mate. They basically grew up together in Clydebank - although Jimmy is a year older. So, Jimmy was my Uncle Tommy's mate to begin with - courtesy of the age difference. But he'd heard about my dad but never seen him. Well, he almost saw my dad on a few occasions - but these occasions were only fleeting glimpses in the night as my dad was 'seen' hurdling hedges in the dark as he made his way home from *'visiting'* girls in the Parkhall area of Clydebank where they all lived. Jimmy nicknamed my dad, *'The Shadow'*, and he decided to befriend him in an attempt to put him on the straight and narrow. And they became best mates.

Jimmy's quest to put my dad on the straight and narrow remains to this day. I'm not referring to late night *'visits'* - my mum sorted that one out. And I'm not referring to the jumping of hedges either - because he was still doing that up until his hip replacements a few years ago. I'm referring to Jimmy just always looking out for dad in the way an older brother would for his wee brother. They think the world of one another and they're both mad Celtic supporters.

So football has always played a part in my family and I know it does within many others. But I was never passionate about the game - even when I worked as a producer in sports programming.

My role at Scottish Television was to oversee the production of all the component parts which make up a programme. That's what a producer does - from deciding on a running order of matches to script writing to editorial content to editing to deciding on which studio guest to invite on any given match weekend. And I was also responsible for directing live programming on air too. But I didn't need to be passionate about the game to do that. I loved the game. But there was no passion for it for me. And I think there's a difference.

My experience meant that I could essentially be dropped into most genres of programming and produce them - because it was producing all of the little parts which made up each programme that I loved to do - that I was trained to do.

I was never interested in appearing on the telly. But I did. I had to when I worked in the newsroom as a journalist and reporter before being asked to move into sport. But being on-screen was never really my thing. My thing was and remains sitting in a dark room editing opening title sequences and feature interviews and cutting them in a way which would be attention-grabbing and entertaining for the viewer. I loved it and I still love doing it as a freelance filmmaker in Bristol. But don't get me wrong - I loved my job at STV and working in the sports department saw me fortunate enough to work alongside many well-known faces in the game - as I've already mentioned.

But my interest in football was to elevate in the late nineties with a request from the Head of Sport. On paper it looked like some kind of demotion. But it turned out to be quite the opposite.

Now, at that time I was working on Scottish Premier League and UEFA Champions League output. And my boss's suggestion caught me a bit by surprise. He asked me if I'd consider producing and directing a brand new football programme which would only cover the lower leagues? He then told me he believed there was a massive demand for lower division football on the television - courtesy of a very different type of passion for the game. I had to take his word on that because I had no idea about who was who in the lower leagues in Scotland at the time. I'd always been working on and producing SPL and UEFA output and so felt a bit nervous about taking on editorial control of a game at a level I wasn't familiar with. I told him I was a bit worried and explained my reasons why. He just told me not to worry and to take a few days to think about it. So I did just that.

My Head of Sport received my answer the following day. It was a sound, *"Yes!"* I agreed because I knew it would be a challenge to get a brand new football programme up-and-running and that it had to have its own unique style and feel - compared to the others which were being aired at the time.

It was one of the best decisions I ever made during my career at Scottish Television. *Football First* was born and from that came an insight through new professional relationships with those who worked in and played in the lower leagues.

There was an openness and a transparency and a genuinely welcoming invitation which I hadn't experienced at a higher level in the game.

The clubs who featured in the programme were always delighted with the coverage - coverage which had for a long time been afforded to the premier league teams - mostly Celtic and Rangers.

These new people in my professional life weren't just representatives of their clubs - but representatives of their communities too. And it was from the streets and alleyways which surround and meander and embrace their respective lower league stadiums that I first experienced what I believe is the original fervour for the game - just the same as in the streets and alleyways which surround and meander near the Memorial Stadium.

Gritty passion born from working class aspirations and dreams. Life might be shit on the streets and alleyways - but there was always the dream at the end of the road or a bus-ride away or a train journey away that promised an excitement which lasted ninety minutes which you shared with hundreds and thousands of others who knew the same streets and alleyways and shops and schools and cafes and more.

Pure passion born from blood as generations of supporters presented new generations of supporters and christened the new faithful to their own families' allegiance and colours founded on those same streets or alleyways - as opposed to those who follow a team from a faraway city because their ninety minutes features world-class players and managers who win success and silver honours by the grace of cash. Some might say that isn't even a true football passion and many will say it's nothing less than glory hunting? But it's probably best I stope there on that one. Helen's an Arsenal supporter. Then again - being a Gunner doesn't make you guilty of hunting for glory!

It was about producing a programme which not only captured the *rough-and-ready* and *blood-and-thunder* nature of the game - but also to capture the gritty and real and true essence of the supporters who stood exposed in the sleet and rain and wind and sun every Saturday. The fans who could walk to the ground because their ground was at the end of their street and that's why they went - because their mothers and fathers and aunties and uncles and grandparents went amassed with so many others before them. That's what I connected with when I began producing *Football First* and that's what I fell in love with - its truth.

And it was that truth which I saw and felt again on that day in 2013 when Helen took me to my first Bristol Rovers match and it's that truth which kept pulling me back for more - even when the football was dire and my back hurt from standing and the pie was nothing less than an unholy abomination wrapped in pastry (you'll find I'll go on and on about this throughout the book and it's very possible I'll attempt to eat one to raise money for charity in 2016) and it was all costing me lots of pennies when I was just starting up my own small business - so I was always *skint*.

I kept going back to The Mem. It just felt right and I also had a strong feeling that I was going to have an incredible experience. So I just went along with the feeling to see where it would take me. And where it took me and where it continues to take me is to a truth which I see and hear and feel when I'm among the *Army of Blue.*

There's a saying down Horfield way - *'We are the Gas. And if you don't understand that - then you don't matter!'*

I don't think that applies only to *Gasheads.* I know that applies to every other lower league football supporter too.

6 GOING DOWN

'We are the Gas. And if you don't understand that - then you don't matter!'

I witnessed the true meaning of that saying on the third day of May 2014. And I'll never forget it.

Season 2013/2014 saw me venture more and more towards the Memorial Stadium every other Saturday. But no away games.

It was still very early days for me and if the truth be told - I was never really a true supporter at this time. But I was being 'drawn in' and enjoying going to home games when time permitted - time which was otherwise being spent doing the best I could to get by in finding work as a freelance documentary filmmaker.

My twelve years with Scottish Television had provided me with a skill set for a job I loved doing and I found myself producing a lot of short films for a client list which featured a lot of NHS organisations. And most of the productions focused on addiction and recovery from the illness.

Now, I essentially had two sets of experience which allowed me to film and edit these films. The first was obviously my experience working in broadcasting. The second was the fact that I was and remain in recovery for alcohol addiction.

Now this is something which I don't need to share within these pages. But for me - the first rule of writing is to be truthful. So it's important to me to be honest and it's a truth within this honesty that's the very reason why I ended up in the West Country and ended up meeting Helen and then ended up falling in love with Bristol Rovers.

I suppose I could tell you a wee white lie? I could quite easily make something up - something fantastical and even bizarrely interesting. But that's not really me and I'm sure by now you've established that there's no way my state of mind is capable of mixing fantasy and non-fiction. And yes I know you're sitting there reading this bollocks and shaking your head with a smile on your face!

So I was in recovery and I'm still in recovery and I'll always be in recovery. It just has to be this way for me now and I'm more than happy with that. I'm not anti-alcohol and I genuinely don't mind being around people who drink. It's just as well because my passions outside of work and my family are BRFC and live music gigs. And these pastimes go hand in hand with the occasional cheeky 'Golden offerings to the Gods'. But it doesn't bother me. And as I write these words - I'm five and a half years sober and I'm quite comfortable in my sobriety. I don't miss it and it's almost as if it's become invisible to me when I'm out and about at matches or concerts.

This new way of thinking is courtesy of the five months of residential rehab I spent in Weston Super Mare in 2010. And it was during that time in that place that I was helped to think in a different way about myself - a way which straighten a thinking process which saw me use alcohol to escape from the world around me.

I won't say any more about my recovery because this book isn't about that. I just wanted to be truthful about why I ended up in Bristol. I moved here immediately after my rehab was completed. And I'm more than happy to be open about it. We tend to have a drink in the bar before kick-off and that's part of the Saturday ritual.

But I do need to say this. I may have once been a successful journalist and producer and director back in the day - but I was also a man scared of life and my place in the world. I never felt as if I belonged and I ended up losing everyone and everything because of alcohol. I lost my wife, my home, my career, my friends and my self-respect. And my rock bottom came in the shape of living in a homeless hostel in Ipswich. And it was in that place - where I almost lost my life - that an intervention took place June 2010 - an intervention which was to see me sent away for the treatment I needed and the beginning of a whole new life with new loves for me.

And one of these many new loves - is the pride I have in being a *Gashead*. And so I don't mind sharing this part of my past with you - because I know it's safe in your hands. It's a safety I feel when I'm with all of you at home or away and I'm sure it's a safety which I'll be privileged to feel for the rest of my days.

I'm also not naive. I know most people find it hard to imagine life without a good few sherries. And I know there's a stigma which still prevails surrounding addiction. But I truly believe the only way to smash the stigma is to be more open about the illness. And that's one of the main reasons why I'm sharing this with you. I've seen so many people suffer alone because they're too afraid to ask for help for fear of being judged by others. And that's not right. And it's not right because a lot of people are struggling with booze. Some you may not know. Some you definitely know.

A few pages ago - I mentioned the player who scored that incredible goal for England against Scotland at Wembley in Euro '96. It was sublime to watch and it remains so for me to this day. And a few pages ago I said I'd mention him at a more appropriate point - so it feels okay to mention him now.

I met Paul in 1996. I was working in the newsroom at the time a few months before my transfer to the sports department.

It was a week night and I was on shift in news. One of the sports journalists came into the newsroom and asked a favour. He told me Gazza was coming in to the building to watch a Rangers match in one of the hospitality suites. Paul couldn't play. He was injured. But he wanted to watch his side play and I'm sure it was a Champions League away game. The sports journalist asked if I wouldn't mind occasionally checking on him to make sure he was okay. And I said no problem.

So, through the my shift - I'd steal myself away from producing the three minute late night bulletin to make sure he was fine and had everything he needed to watch the game. And I found him to be a very quiet and unassuming guy. He was just sitting on a sofa with his mate - Jimmy Five Bellies - and enjoying the game. But he did come across as a bit withdrawn and I've no doubt it was because he'd rather have been playing than watching the match.

A few words were exchanged between the three of us and they were no problem at all. To be honest - I was expecting some kind of mayhem in some shape or form. But it never happened. We chatted and he was very polite and quiet. He didn't give much away - probably a wariness of journalists. And I was okay with that. It was never my intention to intrude or ask questions. We just enjoyed a bit of banter about the match and me being a Celtic supporter enjoying a bit of banter with a Rangers player. He was great.

I consider myself very fortunate to have spent a small amount of time with the man who is arguably one of the greatest midfielders and players the world has ever seen. And his goal against Scotland is testament to that.

But despite his genius on the pitch - as we all know - he's struggled with himself and it was a few years later in my own life that I could identify and empathise with Paul. To understand the horror of active addiction is to experience it. There's no other way. And thankfully - it's becoming more acceptable to talk about it openly.

Paul Gascoigne is one of my footballing heroes. And it takes a lot for a Scot to say that! But he is and I'll never forget all the times I had to endure my stomach tied up in knots every time the ball fell to his feet during an Old Firm Derby - with back straight and his chest out and his arms out as he ran amok in his own gifted way.

I genuinely hope he finds peace from the madness. I managed to find it. But it isn't easy. And it'll be so much harder for him because of who he is. Fame invites a spotlight which shines a darkness on a way out for celebrities. I truly hope he finds peace.

'We are the Gas. And if you don't understand that - then you don't matter!'

Now, back to that day which was the third day of May 2014.

I remember it as being warm and overcast with the occasional breaks of sun and blue sky. And it was a working day for me because I'd been asked to shoot a promotional film for a Bristol-based charity which was overseeing and promoting the city's architectural open day.

So it was going to be a busy Saturday for me as I lugged my kit around the streets and alleyways of my new home town - so I knew there was absolutely no way I could be at the Memorial Stadium for Bristol Rovers' final match day of the 2013/2014 season. And I was a bit disappointed to say the least because this match day was a crunch match day for the blue and white faithful.

The Gas were sitting precariously at the bottom of the League Two table which saw relegation looming over three teams. And we were one of those teams.

The basement battle had become a battle of numbers as we were involved in a numerical dogfight with Wycombe Wanderers and Northampton Town to avoid ending up holding hands with already-relegated Torquay to provide a double-up feast for the Orc Army in non-league football. One point was all we needed to stay safe and out of harm's way.

So it was all eyes on *The Mem* and two other grounds in that tier for us on that Saturday - a day which I'd decided on doing my best to finish filming by 3pm - so I could at least catch the second half and hopefully not witness what hadn't even entered my thought process in the build up to the final match day weekend.

It was weird. The thought of the reality of relegation hadn't really crossed my mind. I know these were still early days as a supporter for me and so I didn't have the passion for the club the way I do now - but even then, the idea that a club like Bristol Rovers could end up playing non-league football for the first time since 1920 just didn't seem to register in my head. It was as if my brain was overriding on assumption that the sums would somehow add up for us because a 'minus' BRFC in the fourth tier of the English game just isn't cricket - even though it's football.

We were at home to Mansfield Town - a town very familiar with our manager, Darrell Clarke, who'd only been our gaffer for a few weeks following John Ward's 'move upstairs' to Director of Football. And it must have all been a bit scary and a wee bit weird for our beloved D.C. - because he was born in Mansfield and he began his playing career with Mansfield Town in 1995 - making one hundred and sixty league appearances over six years for the Stags. So, hardly surprising if he felt he was in a bit of a rut!

So it was on that warm and cloudy and periodically sunny day that I grabbed my kit and caught a bus from Kingswood and into the city centre to do a professional - if not hurried - filming job, before racing up the ground to see the second half of the match.

I had to use public transport in those days because I was still doing my best to get everything back that I'd lost due to alcoholism. So, buses it had to be and it wasn't unusual for some poor sod to end up getting the wrong end of a tripod in their face as I clambered onto a double-decker - laden with cameras and bags - looking as if I was on some kind bizarre training exercise to get me ready for Everest.

Helen told me she'd keep me updated with the score - so I knew I'd be on top of the latest news from the ground as I was weaving my way in and around historic city landmarks whist filming concrete and stone and iron stairwells and the occasional interviewee talking on camera about the unique and colourful history witnessed by thousands of street facades since the departure of the Roman legions.

All great stuff and all the kind of stuff I genuinely enjoy - but not really when it's 2.55pm and one of the most important matches in my new club's recent history is about to kick-off and I'm not there to see it begin - along with ten thousand other supporters - thanks to some bloke called Bernard enthusing on camera about how he choreographs music to water fountains on the harbourside.

Helen's first text arrived at 3.36pm. It wasn't good. Mansfield had taken the lead and Colin Daniel was the culprit. And yet I still remained oblivious to any concern about what might be about to happen. It just didn't seem real to think we weren't going to end up safe and I had absolute faith that our lads would turn it around in the remaining fifty four minutes of match time. So I simply carried on with my final shots before packing up my kit to get ready for my journey to where Helen and Claire and Simon and the rest of my new *Gashead* friends were - the Memorial Stadium on Filton Ave.

I tried to run but couldn't. It wasn't because I was laden with cameras and tripods and bags. I just should've known there was no point in trying to run - because I've known for nearly thirty years that I've only got one leg.

It happened a long time ago when I was growing up in South Africa after my family left Scotland when I was a young boy. But no need to dwell on that now. It's not important. But what is important is what I witnessed when I arrived at the ground. However, it's always with mischievous delight when I announce that I may be the only one in Bristol in recovery for alcoholism who is legless all of the time. Sometimes you've just got to laugh!

So I made my way from Bristol's harbourside and up towards the *Bearpit* - passing the Hippodrome and then Colston Hall and onto Lewins Mead - passing the Christmas Steps and then St James' Priory before arriving at the bus stop at the bottom of Cheltenham Road.

It was still a warm and partially cloudy day as I jumped onto the number 73 bus - but I'm sure it felt a lot warmer than it actually was after not running for ten minutes. And that's what you get for sitting right at the back of the bus. You end up sitting above the engine. Genius move in winter. Not the brightest move in late spring.

The bus ride on Cheltenham and then onto Gloucester Road to Horfield took about twenty minutes and as we grinded our way up the hill - I looked at my mobile phone to see if I'd missed any incoming text alerts from Helen. But there were none. So this could only mean one of two things - we were either ahead after drawing equal and she was too busy celebrating to text me - or the scoreline remained the same as it was when I received her first and only score text. I had a feeling it was the latter. And that feeling began to feel heavy as I disembarked the number 73 bus to cross Gloucester Road to step onto Filton Avenue - then right into the Memorial Stadium.

The sense of heaviness weighted more as I passed through the gates - gates featuring tributes and honours to local rugby players who fell during the Great War - and into the ground which was built on land once known as Buffalo Bill's Field, after Colonel William "Buffalo Bill' Cody's Wild West Show was held there in 1891.

The atmosphere felt really bizarre. I could hear the hum of ten thousand voices as I passed the empty supporters bar behind the Blackthorn End - a hum devoid of any sound of hope - as if the sound of ten thousand voices had flatlined and now all that remained was the monotonic tone of hopeless expectations.

There were a handful of people just wandering around behind the north terrace stand - looking bewildered and silent as only minutes remained for Bristol Rovers to equalise and maintain that scoreline and secure the point to avoid something which had been unimaginable to me at the start of the day.

But it was what I saw seconds later - before reaching the turnstiles - that I'll remember for the rest of my life. There was a group of around a dozen supporters holding onto the steel gates and peering through the gaps in the security fence as they tried to see the final moments of the match. Like me, they didn't have a ticket. But they were holding onto the gate for dear life -

eyes fixed on a game unseen as the colour drained from their faces and tears began to fill their eyes as the realisation of what was about to happen began to rise up from the warm tarmac - on which they nervously stood - and snake around them in a vice-like grip which was only seconds away from pulling them down into non-league football.

And I wondered why they'd all ended on the wrong side of the gate? And my heart sank when the possibility dawned on me that they may have heard from friend's texts or the radio or television about what was looking likely to take place to their club at their ground. So with the match being a sell-out and no way to get in to see the game - maybe they'd been at the gate since kick-off? Or perhaps they'd been at home or at work or out shopping when they heard the news and made their way to the stadium to make sure that they - in their own way - could maybe prevent what was looking like happening from happening as news broke of the very real possibility that history was about to be made at *The Mem* - for all the wrong reasons.

Anchored by their imminent fate - they swayed instead from side to side - still gripping the massive steel gate in a passionate attempt to hold onto not just steel - but a place in the Football League which was now almost beyond their grasp.

So, holding firm they attempted to see through the supporters who were inching closer towards them on the other side of the security steel. These fans kept stopping to look back at the pitch and then turn again to move away from the game which had seen three Bristol Rovers strikes hit the crossbar - with two more unwelcome trinities taking place elsewhere in other parts of the country with Northampton's 3-1 home win over Oxford United and Wycombe Wanderers' three-nil away win against an already-fated Torquay.

And it was that win for the *Chairboys* which put them on equal points to us in the league table - but they sat above us on third courtesy of goal difference.

Regulation time had almost come and gone and it was over. Everyone knew it. It was over and then the referee made it official. It was done.

Bristol Rovers were relegated from the Football League and hearts were broken beneath the scattered cloud and blue sky high above *The Mem*. And it was the 3rd of May - the day after the second day of the same month which went down in Gas history at Twerton Park in 1990. The 2nd and 3rd of May will now surely represent the respective highs and lows for *The Gas* far and wide for years and generations to come. And their closeness epitomises just how intimate the highs are to the lows in the life of a football supporter.

The steel gates were opened and I stood and watched as hundreds of *Gasheads* tried to leave - but then stopped again to look back in some kind of attempt to convince themselves that what had just happened - hadn't really happened and that somehow, someone had made a mistake. But there was no mistake. It had just happened and I slowly moved my way through supporters - some crying and some venting their anger to whoever and whatever would listen.

I didn't consider myself a true *Gashead* at this specific moment in time. I was a supporter of *The Gas* and for me - there's a difference. But as I turned right and onto the thoroughfare which runs beneath with bar windows and the top step of the Blackthorn End - I began to feel as if I was in some kind of vacuum where everything seemed to be still. It felt like you feel when you come across the scene of a horrible traffic collision and there's nothing you can do because you don't know how to help those around you. I felt helpless. And then I felt an intense apprehension about seeing Helen. I felt afraid because I knew she'd be so upset and I also knew there was nothing I could do - nothing I could say.

When I saw her - she was standing with Claire. Shoulder to shoulder. Both had their backs to me and both were staring out and across the pitch as supporters were escaping the stands and running towards the away end - only to be met by six police officers on horseback. It wasn't chaos by any means. I think most people were too shocked to react in a riotous manner - but there were Rovers fans punching obscenities up to the directors box from the north terrace and screaming demands that the board must go and for chairman Nick Higgs to make himself available to answer a few questions about what the hell had just happened and what the hell was now going to happen?

Most supporters knew the answer to those questions. Conference League Football was to be our non-league destiny for the following season and that was that. There was no way it was going to change. Everyone was distraught - but it should never have been allowed to happen in the first place. Teams find themselves in these positions in league tables for many reasons - and yes it's going to hurt.

Promotion and relegation. It's part of the game. And for me - relegation should be at the forefront of every club and every player and every manager's thoughts at the start of every new season - because the one thing that causes even more heartache at these times is the *"What ifs?"* being whispered from tearful fan to tearful fan. Every match should be regarded as a relegation battle in the final day of the season - that way it's pretty much guaranteed that supporters will be saved from tearful whispers.

So we were relegated and the barrage of resentment-in-sound hit the directors' box in a wave of fury. But unless Higgs had acquired access to the Tardis - our final position in League Two wasn't going to change.

The barking of demands by the fans to see and hear from those who run the club - demands justified in my own personal opinion - continued as I slowly edged my way down the stairs and then said hello to Helen and Claire. And they turned and they were both in floods of tears. And it was at that point - that precise moment in time - that something sparked within me and it was if a voice within me said, *"You will follow Bristol Rovers next season and you will do everything that you can to play your own small part in getting right behind the Gas and being part of the fight and stand next to the girl you love at as many games as you can and do your bit to support this team back where they belong in the Football League!"*

Now, before you say or think anything – my answer is a resounding *"No!"* God wasn't speaking to me and telling me I had to become a *Gashead!*

It was a *feeling* I had. And I'm sure I also heard the *feeling* say *"Up the Gas!"* at the end. But I can't swear on that one. And with that - at that moment in time and feeling those words - I now know in my heart that it was the very beginning of the falling-in-love process between myself and BRFC.

'We are the Gas. And if you don't understand that - then you don't matter!'

The fact that it mattered so much - in the hurt I saw in others – was what made such an impact on me. It was the first time I'd ever seen fans so upset in that way and it really did have a profound effect on me. I'd never before supported a team which had suffered relegation. And it was if that horrible experience awakened something within me and wanted to be part of a good fight.

There was no fighting spirit within any of us as we drifted away from the Memorial Stadium on that still-warm day with the occasional splattering of clouds in the blue sky. And then I remembered something that had happened during my time producing *Football First* at Scottish Television in Glasgow. So I shared it with Helen as we walked back to the car in some small attempt to maybe help her see that the day's events might not be that bad? And to my great surprise – she didn't try to punch me in the face when I told her this…

Hibernian FC were relegated from the Scottish Premier League in May 1998. And it was the best outcome they could have hoped for - in my own opinion – and so their following season's matches would feature on the programme I was producing at the time, *Football First*.

Hibs manager Alex McLeish had set about ridding his side of players who were high earners and not delivering on the pitch. Now this was to be expected as he took his squad into the Scottish Football League's First Division - having lost earnings from not playing in the SPL - but he ended up being on a winner.

He took on younger players who were passionate about playing for the jersey instead of weekly wage of thousands. And what he ended up with was a side with fight and passion for results which saw the *Hibees* run riot in the First Division the following season and romp the title to win promotion back into the SPL within twelve months. Does this sound familiar now? I fecking bet it does!

Big Eck was a regular guest on Football First. Nice lad. Ginger too - like me. It might be a Scottish thing - but then again - my grandad's from Norway so I'm more Scandinavian blonde as opposed to ginger. But Big Eck is definitely a ginger. And his team's matches tended to be my multi-camera game of the weekend. And why? Well, it would have been difficult to not afford them that kind of coverage when they were running amok in a three-point-grabbing campaign all over Scotland whilst showboating new talent to boot. Ring any bells?

And with that story true - Helen nodded and agreed that the Rovers had been toiling for a few seasons and the events of the day might just be what the club needed to give itself a sound boot up the arse and shake things up a bit.

And what was to follow, as you know dear readers, was one *helluva* season in the Conference League where we picked up some fine talent - including a true-to-life bearded Pirate!

And there were others to follow and it was to be my first full fixture list of highs and lows as I honoured the voice within myself *"You will follow Bristol Rovers next season..."* and I watched as we fought and grappled with the ugliest teams in world football.

But this time something had changed and the changes came in the shape and faces and beards of lads who were willing to play for the jersey and for one another and for us for all to see that we are indeed Bristol Rovers and we do indeed do what we want and what we wanted to do was get the hell out of *Vanarama Dodge*. And we did. And we did it in style.

7 FEAR THE BEARD

Exeter City v Bristol Rovers
St James' Park, 28th November 2015

It's as you look down at your plate in Wetherspoons in Kingswood on the morning of your away clash against Exeter that you realise your full English breakfast - the large option because the weather outside is cold and bleak and wet and windy - is not really a full English, because for it to be a full English, requires sausages.

So you look across the crowded public house - with air still fresh with stale fumes of lager and lust from the night before - to find a member of staff who can gaze upon your wounded expression and help you find peace from the turmoil within by finding and adding the missing thousand calories from your already overflowing plate.

So as you eat with your loved one and two friends - all adorned in the hallowed colours of the blue and white quarters - you analyse and dissect the fixture ahead within the hours ahead with a bombardment of *what ifs* and *we need's* in a carefully assembled jigsaw of match-tactic-truth with a confident apprehension amid a post-Stevenage sorrow.

Your pre-match analysis features heavily on the new twenty-six year old on-loan arrival from Cambridge who - at six feet four - qualifies with his physical attributes, but yet unseen by Gashead eyes as to whether or not he has the head and boot and 'box of tricks' to qualify his position as a striker. And so you chat among yourselves - in some kind of huddle over empty plates which look more like the aftermath of a massacre, as remnants of bacon fat soak still in tomato sauce - in a conversation which also delves into your new forward's bloodline and it reveals he's Irish and this in itself offers a new kind of hope because there's defiantly one of the things we've been missing and it's that one thing you're hoping new lad Rory Gaffney has brought with him to Bristol Rovers - some luck!

It's almost time to hit the road as an old friend of the friends you're with wanders in as he escapes the brewing madness of Christmas shopping in late November and grabs himself a pint and merrily informs you that the charity shop across the road has three old Rovers jerseys and they're only two quid each and he also says they'd fit you.

"Fit me?" you say. "Yes!" is the reply.

So it's with that, that you hurriedly excuse yourself and put on your jacket - not the thermal wetsuit type required for this kind of weather - and you exit the public house and into the cold and rain to skip across High Street and into the warmth of the shop which was recently scouted by your friends' merry pint-swigging chum.

You wander the racks and rows of clothing - all kindly and recently donated by those who are no longer with us - and your excitement rises as you imagine the delight in acquiring three new, old additions to your Gas football top collection for the bargain price of six pounds. And it's with heightening elation that you see the colours blessed by Irene.

You grab all three at the same time because it's better to be safe, because you don't want someone else grabbing the other two while you're only holding one. It's not that you're selfish. It's just because you're self-nurturing. And there's a massive difference.

So you hold all three aloft on their wire hangers and you then wonder why all of the lights have gone out in the shop as an unexpected darkness descends. The first thought lasts only a split second. But it's a very long split second as you wonder if Forest Green Rovers' man-mountain pie-eating striker - Jon Parkin - has somehow read what you've written in a previous chapter and he's not happy and he's somehow found you in Kingswood and maybe that's why there weren't any sausages on your plate because Parkin had been hiding in the kitchen in Wetherspoons - waiting for his moment to pounce - and he's now followed you into the charity shop and now he's behind you.

But your pantomime of one second insanity is replaced by the reality that you aren't about to be eaten and the true reason why it's now dark in the shop is courtesy of the three circus tents pretending to be football shirts which you're holding aloft. Fit you? Your friends' merry chum was probably correct. But they'd probably only fit you if you ate Jon Parkin.

And with that you exit the charity shop and once again skip across High Steet to return to *Spoons* to deliver two fingers to the still merry pint-swigging friend of your friends before you all wave goodbye and jump into your black Peugeot 308 and start heading south towards Exeter with three hours to go before kick-off at a ground you've never been to before and a place where the opposition has been unbeaten in recent months and so your apprehension rises again as your recent memory of how you felt after your home game against Stevenage comes flooding back and you pray your new Irish striker lives up to the superstitions born from his land of birth.

The wind and rain hammers the windscreen of your car as you cruise down the M5 motorway towards your hope of a victory in the shape of one point.

A single point won away from home would do after what's happened in the weeks and months of Memorial misery - of missing chance after chance and seeing ball after ball lobbed and weighted and flighted into the eighteen yard box with the same outcome over and over again - no heads with height and no score.

And it's with this in mind in the car as you hurtle towards St James' Park that you all also feel a little bit sad following the recent departure of Nathan Blissett, who's just forty-eight hours into a new on-loan move to Lincoln City and might never return. But you hope he does because deep down in your heart you know he's got something very special and as soon as his head connects with his feet then that 'something special' will be unleashed into the beautiful game and you want him to be wearing the blue and white quarters when it happens.

Big Bliss. You know in your very soul that he'll enter hero-status at some point in *Gas* legend. But if he doesn't return then the only way that'll happen is if he ends up signing for *'them down the road'* and scores an own goal when we meet them in League One next season. It's very possible. And you all agree as you sit in the *toastie* warmth of the car - listening to the new Muse CD - that Big Bliss is more than good enough to play for Bristol City and he'd look great in red too.

So there's plenty of time because the weather isn't causing traffic chaos as you speed along towards the 3pm kick-off and your friends in the car – Helen, Claire and Simon - share some memories from *Gas Glory* in days gone by.

You listen as you steer and peer through the rain against glass as places and names and players and managers and fixtures bounce around the cockpit and it's from the front passenger seat where your friend Simon tells you he's been a *Gashead* since he was sixteen. You listen as he shares how he started going to watch Bristol City as a wee boy and how he used to stand on a wall in the east stand. You hear how it was difficult for him to make his own way to the games at such an early age, so he ended up going to watch Bristol Rovers instead and how he fell in love with the club because the fans were better and there was a better atmosphere and it was a true family club.

So you drive and you listen to a *Gashead* telling you a story of old and it's the same story you've heard from some other *Gasheads* who you've met since becoming a supporter of the club. They started watching City - then switched to the one true team in Bristol.

And so the journey continues and the distance between the front of your car bumper and Stadium Way is falling fast, but not as fast as the misery that fell on the Reading faithful on the 16th of January 1999 as one of your passengers (Helen) reminds everyone of Rovers' stunning six second half goals at the Madejski Stadium - seen by three thousand travelling away fans (including Helen) who witnessed Jamie Cureton net four goals and Jason Roberts finish off the hammering with two in the final two minutes of the match.

And it's with memories of that royal rout that your car is filled with laughter and smiles as you start to think about the bar of Twirl which you can see next to you but you decide not to, because if you do there's a good chance you could end up fitting into those Rovers jerseys. So you decide against the additional cocoa high because you're feeling good enough and then you start to feel a lot better as you see the signpost which reads Exeter - Honiton - Yeovil.

The latter fills you with a mixed feeling of dread and relief and joy and you're feeling joyful because you're racing past Yeovil and you're eternally grateful that you don't have to stop, because that's where the dreaded twelve-finger fans live and they're the reason why it's impossible to find any banjos in Bristol. They're all in Yeovil.

The deliverance of relief that your bottom remains intact despite being so close to the place where they wear dungarees with buttons on the back, instead of the front, is a welcome relief and a joyful one for everyone in the car - because it wasn't that long ago that a Yeovil supporter was photographed holding up a sign which read *'It could be worse we could support Bristol Rovers - non league'* when you were relegated at the end of season 2013/2014.

So everyone in the car is now grinning and you are too because Yeovil Town are now facing non-league medieval warfare against the Orc Army in Gloucester next season. It's looking grim for them - hardly a fairytale run-up to Santa coming as they lay prostate in League Two's dungeon. You know it must be cold and dark down there for them - not quite Sleeping Beauty as opposed to Sleeping Ugly - and this fills your Gashead heart with festive cheer, because you know their manager is about as inspiring as a pumpkin and so he'll fit in well with the vegetarian option at the stadium in Nailsworth - but only if he survives the current season.

Your smiles within the car - racing towards what will hopefully be that much needed point - continue as you all share the latest on the fan who made the sign. You've heard he's now allegedly on the run. You've also heard it's alleged he underwent a sex change after you won promotion the following season. It seemed he had to because he'd made himself look a bit ridiculous - although he already looked silly in the photograph - so he had to change his identity. A cheery vice from the back seats reveals how it's believed he now goes by the name Brenda and looks even more ridiculous. And the cheery voice also alleges Brenda will be featuring in a new series of a well-known UK daytime 'chat show' and the episode will be titled, *Karma and Me – The Ugly Truth.*

So the time continues to tick as you arrive in Exeter for the game on which a lot is hanging.

You slowly make your way through roads and alleys and roundabouts and streets from which Victorian terraces gaze down on your black Peugeot 308 which bounces along courtesy of four *Gasheads* revelling in unqualified expectation considering recent results - but that's the way it has to be and that's the way it should be and that's the way it'll always be. Life as a football supporter - hope amid the horror.

And so you park the car not far from the ground and the weather's cleared nicely and the rain has stopped so spirits rise as you wrap yourselves in jackets and scarves and gloves and heat patches and fill your pockets with tickets and chocolate and pain killers - just in case the home supporters have an affinity with the Forest Green players and their passion for biting.

The meandering begins as you weave and turn and walk the winding streets towards the place the Exeter faithful call *The Shed*. And it's as you turn a corner that you see the first evidence that the mighty Blue Army has landed in Devon - an empty can of Thatchers cider balancing precariously on a window ledge just yards from the train station where the *Gashead* invasion began. And as you look up from the can - once filled with liquid aspirations for a slim chance at an away point and an even slimmer chance of pulling a *hottie* in the home stand - you see just why they fondly refer to their home ground as *The Shed*. It's because it's a big shed! But this particular shed is without a particular tool. But that may change because he's currently with Northampton Town and you're sure he's only scored five goals for them so far this season compared to the eighteen he scored when he was with *The Gas* - so it looks like he's found the glory days he felt he deserved.

And so you trundle over the bridge that crosses the railway line and follow Wells Street until you turn left onto St James' Road - all the while unable to take your eyes off the corrugated iron monstrosity which surely must have seated members of the colonial armed forces as they enjoyed watching a game before being shipped out to South Africa to sort out those pesky Zulus in 1879 - to see the remnants of your fellow-away supporters drifting past the security personnel and police who're out in full force to quell any uprising from *The Gas* in the event that the dreaded chicken tikka pie makes an unwelcome appearance.

So it's with Michael Caine's effeminate battle cry in your head that you enter the ground and your eyes fall on the splendour of what your eighteen quid ticket entitles you to. A puddle on a step with no roof overhead and you then become thankful that you'd bought your Superdry anorak in London when you went to watch the Foo Fighters concert which didn't happen because Dave Grohl ended up breaking his leg after losing a battle with some wires and gaffer tape on stage in Gothenburg while doing his best to - in his words, *"Shred some tasty licks for the kids up front!"*

But despite all this you start to get a better feeling of what awaits in this time and in this space and you're not really sure why you feel this way but you do and you share it with Helen and Simon and Claire and you're met with looks of concern which suggest they may be worried about your mental health and that doesn't bother you because you're all *Gasheads* together and you support your team through highs and lows - even though you're struggling on the goals front - and you'll still travel to a far-away place to watch DC's lads play in a big, old shed - so you know you're not the only one who might have mental health problems. Being a football supporter can sometimes require the embracing of a certain type of insanity within solidarity.

The giants arrive on cue - just minutes before the game - and it's with the usual unawareness of their own height that they stand right in front of you and not only block out your view of the pitch - but everything which the sky holds too. So you wonder why that is? And you wonder why it always happens or if it's only you it happens to?

You realise it's becoming a regular occurrence at away games and you start to take it personally and you know it might sound a bit paranoid - but you begin to think there's some sort of steroidal and dark conspiracy which is following your every move away from the west country and they're intent on stopping you from seeing the lads when they mostly play in yellow and you're wondering whether it would be wrong to ask the government to reintroduce a diet lacking in vitamins and minerals to the younger generation to stop the feckers from growing so tall so that a shorter and more 'away-match-friendly' type of fan will be available once you reach pension age - because you'll definitely need this type of supporter then because as you're getting older you're noticing you're getting shorter and the only thing which is growing at great speed and length is hair from your nose and now your ears and it's becoming a highly likely reality that when you qualify for your free bus pass which will afford you a free journey to wherever the hell we'll be playing football - you'll more than likely resemble some kind of hobbit as you stand singing *Goodnight Irene.*

And so you ponder all of this as you remain in your puddle and ponder just how big the erections of tissue and muscle in front of you will be? But by now you're no longer thinking about the inches in height of the supporters standing in front of you in years to come and it's just as well because that would be wrong - even though you're a very open minded kind of bloke. You're wondering if you'll still be able to get a hard-on when you look like you're a property owner in *The Shire*?

So it's nearly time and you stand side-by-side with sixteen hundred other *Gasheads* in *The Shed* as both teams warm up and you wonder if your puddle is actually water because there's an unfortunate waft of 'leaking drain' and it dawns on you that you may very well be standing in sewage? But that particular thought is quelled when you realise there's a very strong westerly wind blowing in and it's blowing in over, into and from the main home stand. And this begs a serious question as to what they actually eat on a Friday night in Devon?

And as you stand amid the aroma - you remember the space on which you're standing used to belong to Lady Anne Clifford in 1654 and she used to rent out the land for the fattening of pigs. So in over three hundred and fifty years - nothing much has changed. It still looks and smells like a pigsty.

It's almost as if time stands still for you as the teams run onto the pitch as a subdued and half-hearted rendition of *Goodnight Irene* drifts from behind the goals in your away end as your stomach starts to turn and the fear hits you again as you nervously look to the pitch - then away to the heads and shoulders beside you and around you and beyond and it's as if you're too anxious to stay focused on the players and where they are because where they are and what's about to happen where they are may be the stage for yet another final curtain on hope - a hope that's been pounding within that half-of-heart which commanded you to stay after the final whistle against Stevenage and applaud your players and manager into the tunnel at the Memorial Stadium.

There's part of you that doesn't want to be where you are because where you are could end up being another place that you never want to return to as the thought of what's about to take place in the forthcoming ninety minutes has to be all-or-nothing as your stomach tightens even more and you become more and more aware as you stare at your boots in the puddle that the rest of the *Gashead* faithful are without their usual sound in song - but you're sure it's there somewhere deep within them and you know it's within you too and all it's going to take to spark the explosion of noise is for your new on-loan striker to run riot against their defence and deliver a three-goal-blow to announce his baptism in blue and white quarters and with his fist raised in defiance and victory - storms towards the *Blue Army* after humbling our opposition to the cries of, *"All hail Gaffney! Rory of the Rovers!"*

But your fantasy in the wind and cold in the away end at St James' Park is sharply interrupted by a man in black as he starts the game with a shrieking blow to begin a first half which sees your players take control from the outset and features an eighteen yard volley from your bearded dynamo - Stuart Sinclair - which is pushed away and yet again makes you question what it is about your team that brings out exceptional performances from opposition keepers?

And the pressure continues and your lads are playing out of their skin as rain falls on skin and you start wondering how Exeter have been unbeaten at home for so many games because they don't look as if they could score at Chasers in Kingswood, let alone *The Shed*.

And still the pressure mounts as again and again you watch your team attack over and over and you can hear the *Gasheads* begin to unite in song as Danny Leadbitter skins a defender and delivers the ball into the eighteen yard area where you see something you haven't seen for so long from a Rovers player and it comes in the shape of the head of Rory Gaffney as he rises into the air and makes the connection with Leadbitter's cross - but his attempt at goal is just inches wide and that's when you exhale a sigh of relief because you've just seen what you've been hoping to see for so long - a player who can command the air space above the oppositions eighteen yard box.

It's such a relief to see him reach the ball and it's such a relief to stand staring skywards in the cold and rain and wind as you feel your apprehension diminish and the tautness of your stomach muscles lessen as you become aware that he can do what you've all been hoping he can do since hearing about his arrival and discussing it over breakfast – the breakfast which began sausage-less.

It's with only a few minutes of the first half remaining that Simon nudges you and suggests an early expedition through the masses of other singing and bouncing *Gasheads* to attain the *Holy Grail* of hot and steamy respite from the chilly wetness that is the away end. And it's a respite that can only be found in a plastic cup filled with burning Bovril.

So you both edge yourselves ever-closer to the corner of the ground through the heaving and chanting *Blue Army* - singing out loud to those wearing the soaking yellow away strips of BRFC as they twist and turn beneath the floodlights - to finally get to the serving hatch where you buy your cups of steaming liquid.

It's as you wait to be handed the beverages that you notice an ominous figure standing to your left and he's ominous because you can't see his face as he's wearing a balaclava - but you can see he's smiling and his eyes are smiling too so you smile back and hope he isn't smiling because he's some kind of masked, deranged madman on the run from the police. And if he is on the run from the police - he's not hiding in the best spot - because the police headquarters for the match is sitting directly above him in what can only be described as a portacabin in the sky - plonked on top of the Bovril corner shop.

So you weave and dodge your way back to your allocated puddle and do the very best you can to avoid splashing the liquid Bovril lava onto yourself and others, because losing your own skin can be sore and causing others to lose their skin can also be sore - when they punch you in the face after you've played your part in them losing their own upper epidermis. And skinning is still taking place on the pitch because Danny's still playing a blinder.

So the interval comes and goes and you know something is going to happen because you can feel it and so can everyone else because your lads are running rings around this lot and the inevitable has to happen.

You feel your knees start to tremble and there's a slight form of hyperventilating going on with your breathing - as if some kind of psychic part of you knows what's about to happen but your conscious mind won't allow you to know but your body knows and it's reacting to what your psychic mind is telling it and you wished to feck they'd tell you too.

You're witnessing Ollie Clark's effort clip the top of the crossbar and their keeper parrying Gaffney and a Matty Taylor strike ruled offside - so you know it's coming.

And it comes. And it arrives with the man who looks like a pirate and who is a *Pirate* and he never stops running and it's likely he's broken some kind of record for receiving the *Man of the Match* award at the Memorial because his work rate is faultless and he always gives everything during the regulation ninety and he gives even more to the fans because he always makes time to chat and say hello and this is his first season in League Football and he deserves to be playing at this level because he picked up Billy Bodin's square ball a few yards outside of Exeter's area and struck it with sublime perfection and keeper Olejnik didn't stand a chance and you watch in cold wet ecstasy as Stuart Sinclair's 82nd minute right footed shot ends up in the top left hand corner of the goal.

Thunder. Not from the sky. Thunderous rapture from the BRFC end as your fists punch the air as you scream to the black sky above as the rain pelts your face and it tastes like sweet nectar from celeste as the roar from the *Blue Army* silences the red of *The Shed* in a sound of a thousand sounds and one of those sounds is you screaming to the Gods above, *"I WANT A FECKING BEARD!!!!!!"*

And as you turn your gaze downward from the heavens you see your hairy star adorned with number twenty four racing towards you from the far end of the pitch where he scored with his arms reaching out towards you as every other player chases him down to the moment he slides on his arse just yards in front of sixteen hundred faces filled with relieved elation. And it's defender Tom Lockyer who you see reach *The Pirate King* first and raise him aloft to the thousand sounds of the away end - like an offering of gold to the *Pirate Gods* above the *Blue Army*.

The noise is deafening as song is sung over and over as *Goodnight Irene* rises far and wide and then falls again with the rain across St James' Park to christen *The Gas* and sodden any flame of hope of maintaining an impressive home run for *The Grecians*.

But there's still eight minutes to go and eight minutes is a lifetime when you're singing and jumping around because you see them running at you now - wave after wave of attack as your side can't keep hold of the ball and the high of just a few moments earlier begins to crash as you once again feel your stomach tighten and your knees tremble as you start to hop from foot to foot as the symptoms of your psychic mind once again jump ahead into time and space to see what you can't yet see - but you know is coming. And it does.

It comes in injury time as you're silenced by their equaliser and it's a silence you feel and it hurts as you gaze down at your puddle as the rain splats the back of your hood like a drumroll to an executioners calling. And you don't know what to do. You don't want to look up to see what you can hear coming from the Exeter fans. So you just stare at your puddle and wait for the noose.

You'd all said you'd be happy with a point. So why aren't you happy? You're not happy because you've just watched your side play the best they've played in a long, long time and you didn't expect it to be that way. You'd have taken the point based on recent match performances but the performance you've just witnessed was a winning performance. Your team deserved all three.

And so still in dark the thousand shadows exit the away end in a silent congregation which shuffles along through a thousand puddles where anxious hope once stood. And slowly-slowly does the mass funnel towards a single file which emerges from *The Shed* and dissipates into the Devon darkness to find cars and trains and buses which will play their part in the long journey home.

And you're one of them. With stiffened legs and feet you hold her hand and walk together down St. James Road and then right onto Wells Street and then up onto Devonshire place where you parked your car - while all the way you both feel as if someone gave you the lottery and then took it back again.

Your two friends arrive a few seconds later and you all strip off jackets and scarfs and gloves and heat pads and jump into the car with drinks and crisps and sandwiches and chocolate. And as the engine starts and the headlights light the beginning of the long road ahead - you turn on the radio to hear the post-match reaction which precedes your own in-car-post-match reaction and the verdict is unanimous.

You all agree that you should've won but it didn't happen - but what did happen was a performance worthy of delivering justified excitement for your next match at *The Mem*. And that's what it's all about. You win some. You lose some. You draw some. And if you can find something positive - no matter how small - in the latter two, then that's all that's needed to keep that small spark alive in your heart for your club. That's enough for you to enjoy doing it all over again.

It's that remaining half-of-heart which commands you to applaud your team and your gaffer as they walk off the park following another result which broke the other part of your heart. That's what makes you a true supporter. That's what makes you faithful and true and that's what makes you a *Gashead*.

8 TRUST

"In football, there is no definite lifespan or timespan for a manager. After a while you start smelling of fish. The other week it looked as if I was stinking of Halibut"

More unique and rare wisdom from Ian Hollway - but there's nothing fishy about our current manager. And I'll go so far as to say he's a bit hot!

Now, I know I may get a lot of stick for saying that - but it's true. I reckon we've got the sexiest manager in the world of football and that includes Jose Murinho.

But it was hardly ecstasy for Darrell Clarke just a few weeks into his managerial reign at the Memorial Stadium. It must have been awful for him to be at the helm when we were sent down last year.

I cannot imagine what it must have felt like for the man from Mansfield to stand in the dugout in front of the Dribuild Stand and watch his lads - who're our lads - fall to one goal from a team which hails from his place of birth - a goal which sent him and the team and the club and all of us to a place we really didn't want to go.

But it happened on that day and what also happened on that day was the sight of a manager in tears on the pitch and being consoled by a supporter - one of our own looking out for one of our own.

Who in their right mind would want to be a football manager? Hero-worshipped when it's all going to plan and crucified when it falls apart. But let's afford no blame to D.C. in the events which unfolded on the 3rd of May 2014 and the consequences of those events.

Clarke's arrival at Rovers in June 2013 was as assistant manager to John Ward and it was to prove the right selection for the Bristol club - but only if you believe that Ward and the board were gifted with the blessing of prophecy.

Darrell's experience as manager of non-league side Salisbury City meant he was probably the only man with a ready-made skill-set to undertake the job that lay ahead in the months which followed that awful day. So even though it was disastrous for the club and everyone associated with the club - understatement of the year - at least we had the gift of Darrell Clarke's experience to look to as we began looking ahead to fixtures being played on surfaces which looked more like carefully detailed film sets for a new movie blockbuster about *The Somme*.

To be honest - I think most managers would have done a runner. But not Clarke. He's not the type and you can see why he's not the type. He's the type of young manager who can be relied on to stand his ground and defend the trench to the bitter end. And it's with that steadfastness and resolve that he also blends a genuine passion for the club and 'us lot' who stand in the terraces - sometimes with our heads in our hands. And it's the combination of these attributes which I admire about the man.

I saw these in Darrell after we were hammered 4-1 at home by Newport last month. It was awful to see and we were still chasing that elusive second home win in the league. I can honestly say that - apart from that relegation day in May last year - it was the angriest I've seen Rovers supporters in the Blackthorn End and adjacent stands.

Bristol Rovers fans are proud of a lot and we're especially proud of standing true until the ninety has come and gone.

Unlike supporters of another club in Bristol - we stay 'til the end. And that is a genuine fact. But that was to change slightly on the 24th of October when quite a few supporters began leaving the ground before the final whistle in a fury – in a rage which also remained with the Rovers supporters who did decide to stay in order to vent their anger at what they'd just witnessed.

Now it's really unusual to witness *Gasheads* leaving early and especially unusual to witness blue and white quarters fans barracking the players and manager with boos and sweary words. But it happened that night. And I joined-in in my own way to express my dismay at what I'd just witnessed.

I kept my hands in my pockets and didn't applaud them off the park. I didn't leave. I just stood and watched them in disbelief at what had just happened at the hands of Newport.

It was then that I witnessed why I really like our gaffer.

D.C. walked towards the stand and as he got closer - he half-raised his hand and with his head bowed he acknowledged to all of us that he knew what we knew and that it wasn't acceptable.

He made himself available to apologise and in doing so - I knew it was a genuine apology. He didn't have to do that. Most managers don't. They just storm off the pitch and race past their fans. But not Darrell. He offered his apology in person in front of the Blackthorn End and that - to me - shows he genuinely cares - not just for his squad or results or the club - but for all of us too.

I'm quietly confident he cares about how we feel and how we feel means something to him. And it's that very empathy for us which tells me that this man is going places and I truly hope he stays with us for a long time before he decides to explore these other places - because in my own humble opinion I reckon we've got the best manager in the league.

He may not always get it right - but who does? I don't. Do you? So why should he be any different? And anyway (I'll speak for myself here), who the hell am I to question his team selection and tactics?

I'm not a professional football manager. He is. So I'm hardly qualified to question anything he does before, during and after a match. It's his job and I'm very confident he gives his all at all times. But it is fun when we've got a few minutes of a game remaining and he decides to throw on Big Bliss and my own head falls into my hands as I cry, *"Why, why, why?"* But as I've said before - Nathan will deliver something unique towards Rovers' success. And now it's looking more likely that his departure may now be his gift to our club.

And it's with a heavy heart that I say that - but not as heavy a heart when I see him warming up near the dugouts. But it's with complete truth that I say to you that I remove my tongue from my cheek and say I'll miss Big Bliss and I'll always be a fan – but I'm not quite sure why?

Darrel's got it right. And what I mean by 'right' is his will to win for his club - for our club. And that matters more to me than winning every single game. And I know I can say that because no team wins every single game - unless it's a team financed by billions which features players out of touch with the reality of the lives of most of the supporters in the stands. That's not what being a football supporter is about for me. I'm sure it is for others. But not for me.

Don't get me wrong - I love seeing our lads win and I hate it when we lose - but as long as we go down fighting and giving our all - then that fires a desire to keep coming back because it's more about passion than results at times. And we had our time in proving that true. And it was Darrell Clarke who led that passion as he took us - thousands of us - to a very dark place with an unspoken promise that he'd bring us back again. And he did.

But I'll leave you with this final thought - for this book - regarding our gaffer…

There's still one thing that'll never escape me when it comes to our manager and it makes me smile every time I see him. I think he looks as if he could be an additional cast member in the hit American seventies sitcom - *Happy Days*.

Clean cut with boyish good looks - I can quite easily see Darrell playing a part alongside Henry Winkler who played *Fonzie*. And it's with that in mind that I now - with much delight - take you back in time to the 15th of August 2015.

We'd just clinched an incredible 95th minute Ellis Harrison away goal against Yeovil and our travelling fans were also celebrating escaping with their bottoms intact when Clarke was interviewed on the radio to give his post-match thoughts on the game. And it was during this on-air analysis that our manager asked the reporter, *"How did them down the road get on?"*

Darrell was referring to Bristol City who'd been playing at home against Brentford. And upon hearing that City had lost 4-2 he replied, *"Happy days!"*

Now, as you can imagine - this didn't go down very well with *them down the road* because this was the first time they'd been referred to as *them down the road* and that's now unlikely to change. And their manager Steve *Super-Steve* Cotterell wasn't happy either.

This all made me laugh out loud at the time. *"Happy Days"* from the man who looks like an extra from same-name sitcom. And I mean that with the upmost respect.

Darrell Clarke. He's our Bristol Rovers FC gaffer and it's in him that I trust.

9 AWAKENED

Dover sits in Kent on England's south east coast and it will now always be a very special place for me - because it was in a place not far from the chalky cliffs that I fell in love with Bristol Rovers.

Dover has always been a focus for people leaving and entering Britain. And I had no idea - before arriving in the ferry town - that I would enter as a BRFC supporter and be leaving as a *Gashead*.

This may all sound a bit soppy for some - but it was in a small ramshackle football ground that I awakened to something within my own hurt and it was a realisation that I was hurting for a reason - and that reason is something only a proper *Gashead* or any other true football supporter will understand.

I have many fond memories of the forty eight hours we spent on that away-match weekend. And I'd like very much to share them with you now - because each and every one of them played their own part in my own awakening of me being part of something truly special. But it was one specific moment in time which was to spark the beginning of an incredible journey which I know I will endure and hold dear for my remaining days.

Dover. So much was to happen in the run-in to that match weekend and it was a journey like no other.

Now, I've been around a bit and I've done things and seen things and been places and met people up until that point in time - but nothing like following *The Gas* down from the Football League and into the Conference to find something we'd lost - something we were then to find again in non-league football and it was a something which inspired a team and thousands of supporters to descend on the Memorial stadium and to other grounds - far away and beyond and across England to win it back again. Unity.

So it was with pride and passion and faith and the truth of believing we would do everything we could to play our own part in the revival of our club that we stormed the Conference in a way which delivered a thunderous announcement that we were intent on a return to the Football League in a lightning strike of blue and white fervour aimed upwards at a return to Wycombe Wanderers - and the rest.

They played their part in our demise - just had we had also played a part in our sending-down. But we were going to show them that we don't stay down when we're down. We get up again and when we do - you'd best take us seriously. That's the wise option because behind the will to stand again and fight is generations in blood of blue of the *Gas Army* - nurtured along the banks of the River Avon and passion anointed in Thatchers.

It was game-on and what a game it was. Rovers supporters descended on their club like never before to get right behind their side. You would have thought a club relegated to the

Conference would have suffered supporter casualties as only the die hard and true remained to follow the team? And that was truth with the Blue Army. Only the die hard and true remained to follow Darrell Clarke's men into the abyss of non-league football. But all *Gasheads* are die hard and true - so thousands and thousands of us followed our team into an unknown not known for ninety four years.

This was surely unique in English football. Some teams in the divisions struggle to take a hundred fans to away games. Some can only manage forty supporters when they're on the road. But no more of Bristol City. Bristol Rovers were on the march and we set the Conference League alight.

From match day one to Wembley - our support never faltered. Attendances at our home ground actually increased with an average of between five to seven thousand fans. We didn't just put the Conference to shame. We put a lot of league clubs to shame too. And what was to happen away from our home ground was to leave other clubs stunned as a mass of blue and white history fell on faraway places.

Woking FC had to shut the gates on us. Can you believe that? Although there was an administrative *Cardinal* sin regarding tickets - it still didn't change the fact that the Kingfield Stadium in Surrey ended up bursting at the seams with *Pirates*. Screams and shouts of hundreds of *"Arrrrrr"* could be heard crying from our own seafaring brothers and sisters from the other side of the steel gate - as we ourselves screamed in horror at having to endure watching ninety minutes of our lads having to play on a pitch which was clearly being readied for a moon landing photo shoot. But we didn't care. We were on a treasured rampage - always friendly in high spirit - which was a great advertisement for non-league football.

We know this was true. Bristol Rovers were under the media spotlight and that was fair play. Darrell Clarke was managing more than a side when he guided us in and through and out of the abyss - he was guiding the only club in Bristol with a true history in and through and out of the abyss. And that history comes amid the supporters of *The Gas*.

This isn't just a football club. This is a way of life for those Bristolians who don the blue and white quarters. It's a family. And we remain with our family through thick and thin.

Our pride has always been true. And this truth was proven when we remained with our club during that season. There were no deserters. In fact, I think our club's following grew because of the events on the 3rd of May in 2014. And that's something to be proud of. And with the blessing of hindsight - it's almost as if it had to happen. We had to hit a rock-bottom to get well again. Sometimes that's what's required to get everything back on track. And I say that based on my own personal experiences in life.

Bristol Rovers had been floundering in league football for several seasons in the run-up to relegation. I saw the tail end of that and heard about the rest from other supporters who've been with the club since birth. They'd been uninspired for so long but continued to follow their team because their team was their life and that's what you do when you're a true supporter - you support your side in the good and in the bad - because it's in the bad times that you remember the good times and the great times and you continue to follow and as you follow you beg as you pray to something unseen for a resurrection of the glory days which saw legends born and scorelines held aloft - scorelines with bylines like *'We Thumped 'Em at Trumpton'* in December 1992 when Channing and Stewart and Saunders and Taylor inflicted the second massacre at Twerton in as many years.

Days to be proud of. Days to be proud to stand by BRFC until we see them again. And we did. And we saw the emergence of unity and pride and passion for our club as we won and won and won again - over and over while on the road and at home.

The Memorial stadium would host live television coverage because the broadcasters knew Rovers at home would guarantee viewers at home. And I know what I'm talking about - courtesy of my career with Scottish Television sport in a past life.

It's not just about the fixture. It's also about how it looks on screen. And albeit our home ground isn't Emirates or Old Trafford - it does afford a capacity crowd of over ten thousand screaming voices and it's that kind of atmosphere which broadcasters look for too - along with the fixture taking place on the pitch.

It's the event as a whole which entices high definition television cameras. And we were becoming very familiar in acquiring the *'wholeness'* of each event as we put ball after ball in the back of the net to the deafening sound of thousands of voices in blue and white song.

In television *'speak'* - we were sexy! We already knew that. But our modesty amid our pride has prevented us from sharing that with the football world. We don't stock XXXXXXL in our club shop - unlike '*them down the road!*'

And sexy doesn't just apply to the *Blue Army*. It's the same for our squad. Our lads leave *Gas* wives and girlfriends and daughters and sisters and grannies and some boyfriends filled with desire and lust as they emerge from the tunnel to do battle for the one true team in Bristol. I know this to be true. I'm one of them.

And out of the tunnel - during our Conference campaign - emerged new faces of players who fitted right into our aesthetically pleasing family. Names like Taylor, Leadbitter and Sinclair. Not just new squad members - but players with chiseled features and athletic physiques whose passion to play for the jersey shone like fire in molten steel and melted the hearts and underwear of many a *Gashead*.

(I may have been a bit enthusiastic with that last paragraph. I might have to change it. My insider tells me Mansell isn't happy about being toppled from the squad's '*Horfield-Hottie Top-Ten*' by Sinclair. But I must maintain my journalistic integrity and pen only the truth - the way I've maintained every other page of words within these pages. Sorry Lee.)

So we're an attractive live option for the broadcasters and we were doing an amazing job on the pitch too. It was all coming together and the kick up the arse had worked wonders. No more uninspired performances from times recently passed. We were running amok. And we were all loving it.

Love. It's true what they say when they say love hurts. It hurts because you care so much. And it can hurt a lot. If you didn't care then it wouldn't hurt. But when it does hurt - that's when you know you're in love.

And it hurt a lot in that late afternoon in Dover on the 18th of April this year...

Helen and I had decided to travel to the south east port town the day before our away game with *The Whites* - a game which would see us clinch top-spot in the Vanarama Conference if events elsewhere also went our way.

Barnet were sitting top and just above us in the league table - but only by one point. So it was a massive match and to take three points at the Crabble Athletic Ground would've seen us go into the final match of the season at our Memorial Ground with an incredible chance to win title honours at home. But we were sure Barnet had other ideas.

So we arrived in Kent late on Friday night and just decided to stay in the room of our cozy Bed and Breakfast hotel - which was about a five minute walk from the ground - and indulge in eating a fine array nibbles selected from Marks and Spencer. *Posh Gas!*

We did indulge in something else before turning out the lights - but I've done my very best to maintain a 'family reading' ethos regarding the content of this book. So I'm not sure if I should divulge what we indulged in beneath the freshly washed linen of the king size duvet as a subtle lamp-lit glow caressed our touching silhouettes? What? Yes please do - I hear you say? Oh! Okay then! We swore ourselves to sleep because there was a railway line just outside our window!

A morning blessed with sunshine welcomed us both to a new day and it was with much excitement that I put on my first-ever *Gas* jersey. I'd tried my best to get a quarters top - but the medium size which fits my svelte and muscular physique was out of stock everywhere - so the away top it had to be. And I was delighted with it.

Now that was - up until that point - really unusual for me. I've worn the colours of another team and I now know that I only wore them - I didn't feel them when I wore them. But I felt the colours of BRFC on that morning and it felt incredible. And it still does when I wear our colours - because it's not about the colours for me - it's about what the colours stand for. And by the 18th of April 2015 - the colours of BRFC had become to mean something very special to me. And it was only going to be a few hours before I realised just how important the colours were for me...

We got ready and jumped into the car and headed down to the seafront for breakfast before making our way to the *Cricketer's* pub where fellow away supporters had been invited by the owners of the establishment. But first-up had to be a full English to get us charged up for the stress and pressure that lay ahead.

We were both really nervous as we parked the car and took a stroll along the pebbled beachfront before finding a place to eat.

It was such a beautiful morning and the sun was breaking through the clouds as we walked to the sound of the sea along the spot of shore which launches the world's most famous swim.

We took a few pictures on our mobile phones and uploaded them onto the *Gas* Facebook page - accompanied by posts which read something like, *'Gas Invasion Has Landed'* or something along those lines and then enjoyed breakfast while chatting to a few locals who wished Bristol Rovers well in our game against their own. And that will always remain with me.

It wasn't the first time we'd come across friendly natives during our Conference campaign. It happened all the time and it's testament to the non-league game and everyone involved in football in the lower leagues. We met so many lovely, friendly people during our away weekends. Genuinely welcoming - they played a massive part in our incredible experience during our 2014/2015 season. So I'd just like to say thank you. Thank you very much.

We met some of the best supporters of the beautiful game during that time. Genuine working class people like ourselves who get by and whose passion sees them follow their teams wherever they go - like ourselves - whenever they can afford it. Thank you so much and we'll hopefully not be seeing you again soon. But it would be great to see you up here with us at some point. So hurry up and join us. Yeovil have got a spot up for grabs!

So we left the seafront and made our way up to *Cricketer's* and the place was bouncing. Hundreds of *Gasheads* had packed the pub and the beer garden and there was a festive atmosphere as *Blue Army* songs were sung out loud as queues for pints and burgers and hot dogs got longer and longer - to the point where I don't think they had enough staff to cope - because the *Gas Invasion* was indeed truly underway and it wasn't long before we all departed the pub and started to make our way up the hill on foot to the place where ninety minutes of football awaited - ninety minutes which could deliver the perfect result going into the final match day at the Memorial Stadium.

The origin of the Crabble Athletic Ground dates back to 1894 - and it looks it. But I love these places. I'd rather stand and watch a game at these grounds than go to Wembley to be perfectly honest. It's as if football dreams of glory from past times still echo silently amid the almost-dilapidated and decaying remnants which once sheltered people like us from the elements as they stood and cheered their own teams to victory.

I find these venues captivating. And it was in this rusting reminder that we amassed to get right behind our own lads and when Ellis Harrison volleyed in the close range opener after Big Bliss headed down a Chris Lines free kick in the 64th minute - I'm surprised Crabble didn't turn into rubble considering the amount of jumping up and down that was going on. We went nuts! And for the next twenty four minutes - there was blue song over the white cliffs of Dover!

Silence. Silence fell on the blue song in the 88th minute when Ricky Modeste equalised. He hadn't read our script. The silence was heavy. And that's when I felt it. It hurt. And it continued to hurt until the referee blew the final whistle after five minutes of added time. Seven minutes of hurt. But the hurting didn't stop. It got worse.

It got worse as we all walked out of the ground and away from what had just happened. But every step I took as I walked away couldn't distance me from the pain I was feeling.

Barnet had only managed a 1-1 draw at Kidderminster - so we'd only been a few minutes away from being able to touch clinching the title. A win at home on the final day would've guaranteed that. But no. It wasn't to be. It was going to have to be done the hard way. It was going to have to be the *Gashead* way. And it hurt.

In silence we marched away from Crabble and I couldn't speak. It hurt to talk. Helen couldn't speak either and neither was anyone else as we shuffled away. It was like a death march down a hill and it was horrible. We'd been so close - just two minutes away from a celebration fired-up by a reasonable assumption. But no. Not this time.

It really hurt because the prospect of play offs was too much to bare at that single moment in time. Memories of that day on the 3rd of May 2014 came flooding back and we'd fought so hard to get out of the place we'd been sent to on that day. And we'd been so close to pretty much guaranteeing we'd get back into league football until Modeste appeared. I just felt like crying.

And then something happened within me. It was like some kind of awakening to a truth I was unaware of and once again I felt something deep inside me say something - and this time it said,

"It hurts because you care. It hurts because you love"

And then the pain lifted. Among the grieving *Blue Army* beside me and in front of me and behind me - the pain lifted because it was at that moment that I realised I was a *Gashead*. A proper *Gashead*. I cared about the results and the players and the managers and the club and most of all – my new family. And I started to smile with pride. And I haven't stopped smiling since...

10 GOING UP

"I was looking down to my right to see Lee Mansell being swamped by his Bristol Rovers team mates just seconds after his penalty hit the back of the net to return us to the Football League. My relief was immense. I turned to see my girl. She was in floods of tears. And the memory of her joy will be one of the most endearing memories I'll ever have."

The day at Wembley needs no match report. It happened. We were there. It was an incredible ending to an incredible season. And most of you reading these words were probably there too.

Your memories of that moment on that day will - I'm sure - be forever special in your own minds and hearts of white and blue. And so you don't need me to let you know what happened on that glorious day on the 17th of May 2015. But I'd like to share a bit about our experience and I hope that's okay with you…

There was still a lot to do to reach the final after conceding the draw in Dover. But if my memory serves me well - it all went according to plan because we didn't concede a single goal after the final whistle at the Crabble Athletic Stadium in Kent - but we did go on a goals rampage and scored ten in three matches before arriving for our Conference Promotion Final against Grimsby Town at Wembley.

Ten goals in three games. The first batch took place at our home ground the week after Dover. And once again there was a capacity crowd as the league title with automatic promotion and avoiding the play offs was still arithmetically possible.

We were up against Alfreton Town and we really didn't expect them to be a pushover. They needed a point or points to avoid relegation so we were expecting some kind of fight and it just increased everyone's nerves. It's kind of like that being a *Gashead*. Nervy. Sometimes you're up. Sometimes you're down. Sometimes your high and sometimes times you're low. But most times you're experiencing all of that at the same time in some kind of twisted, stomach-churning and manic flatline.

Blackthorn End season ticket holders receive a free defibrillator with their welcome pack and instructions on how to use it - on themselves. That's how bad it can be being a *Gashead*. But I've heard they're going to be banned at the ground following the use of one during a skirmish between a fan and a vendor over a chicken tikka pie. And those who witnessed the affray said it was shocking. Not the use of the defibrillator during the altercation. They were referring to the pie.

Barnet remained only one point clear above us and they just couldn't afford to slip-up at home to Gateshead. So it was hearts in mouths stuff yet again and if you're a football supporter true - then you know what I'm talking about. And if you play for Forest Green Rovers - then you'll know what that tastes like.

We scored first thanks to Jake Gosling. Barnet then scored at their ground – *The Hive*. Then Ellis Harrison netted our second followed by a third from Matty Taylor. But Barnet went 2-0 up just minutes into their second half and it was fair to say they were unlikely to concede anything at home to a Gateshead side sitting mid-table and with nothing to really play for - unless some of them knew the meaning of *babber* or were conceived inside *Chasers*.

So with the League Title and automatic promotion pretty much guaranteed to Barnet - we decided to put some goal scoring practice in for the play offs. We had to do something because Alfreton hadn't really turned up and we were becoming convinced they were actually Bristol City in disguise - on a masochistic day out to indulge in massacre number three!

So our lads scored another four because we were all there watching them and the match had become kind of pointless so they must have thought they better do something to kill the time and keep us happy and also keep themselves warm and not risk pulling anything and the best way to do that is to keep passing the ball to one another and pop a few in because it just sounds fabulous when ten thousand *Gasheads* hit the roof in ecstasy. And that's what they did. A second for Taylor. Then Mansell. Then Monkhouse. Then Parkes. Bliss. No, not Big Bliss. He didn't score. He wasn't with us at this time. I meant bliss as in joy, happiness or euphoria - none of which are synonyms for the Bliss who's now on loan to Lincoln City.

So it all came to an end on that day and our seven goal thrashing of Alfreton saw them relegated and sent down to an even deeper abyss - National League North - and we finished second behind Barnet for our place in the Conference Play Off Semi Finals. And I was okay with that. I'm not sure why? I just remember I felt quite calm about the whole ending. And so was Helen and quite a few other *Gasheads*.

This is going to sound strange (no stranger than a lot of the stuff you've already read) but a lot of us just seemed to believe we'd qualify quite comfortably over the two legs of the semis against Forest Green Rovers and we weren't really sure why? I think it's because we were all subconsciously aware that good always tends to prevail over evil...

The first leg saw us away to FGR and the match took place at the *New Lawn* in the Shire of Nailsworth on the 29th of April.

The *Shire* of Nailsworth - as I mentioned within earlier pages - sits nestled amid the rolling fields and undulating hills within the *Mordor* of Gloucestershire.

Many people who return from visiting this place always say it has a kind of magic about it. And I'd put money on it being black magic.

Now I have to be a bit careful here because FGR are currently sitting second in the non-league division right below us. And that in itself is a scary thought. Imagining their red eyes peering up through the *New Lawn* at us - at me - is hardly the lavender required for a peaceful night's sleep. But I'm quietly confident we're going to surprise a few folk this season and reach the play offs ourselves. So if they do jump in then I'm sure we'll have qualified to jump out and that presents two breathtaking outcomes for us. The first is we're safe from harm's way. The second is we'll be able to look forward to massacre number three in a League One Bristol Derby.

But back to the *New Lawn* where we were up against Forest Green Rovers. It was a great night to be honest and the pre-match atmosphere was strangely calm with expectations high that we'd win. That was the universal feeling among the blue and white faithful - including Merv.

Merv BRFC Harris and his partner Vicky are the personification of our club. They attend every home and away game and a lovelier couple you will not meet.

Merv is a human Rovers encyclopedia and I've learned a lot

from him about the history of the club during many conversations we've all had together before and after games. And we indulged in yet another as we enjoyed a drink and looked around to see what they had on the food front. It's a vegetarian club so the options were limited to tofu and lentil burgers. Merv wasn't interested. He's a fish and chips kind of guy and he should really be writing a book about the best Chippy in England because - by the sounds of it - he's enjoyed fish and chips from almost every Chippy in the country whilst following our team on the road. Now that's a true supporter for you! *Grouper Gas*!

So the game commenced and it was horrific to watch - but it was fun in a bonkers kind of way. The referee was clearly vegan with the amount of bookings he didn't give FGR for grievous bodily harm directed at our lads - and all the time there was a giant inflatable willy being thrown up in the air in our end. And whenever it fell out of reach of *Gas* hands and landed on the grass behind the goal - hundreds of Rovers voices sang, *"We want our willy back!"* It was all very funny amid the terrible assaults taking place on the pitch. And it got funnier when our supporters added to their choral song list with, *"We want pies! We want pies! We want pies!"* But the pork wrapped in pastry never arrived.

Madness. But it was to get madder. As if the affray on the park and a giant anti-gravity erection wasn't mad enough - out popped a few Bristol City supporters who'd been hiding in among us lot. And they made their appearance at the best possible moment...

It wasn't long after our very own Matty Taylor netted a blinder from an almost impossible angle early in the first half that they made their unfortunate decision to nail their true colours to the mast. Taylor's strike was perfect and our end erupted as our striker - signed from FGR before the start of that season - celebrated with arms open in front of our stand which was packed with screaming *Gasheads* and floating genitalia.

It was when we all started singing *Goodnight Irene* that the City voices - clearly a result of not taking their medication – began mocking our hallowed anthem. And this was to see them silenced by much bigger and much harder supporters who were standing right next to them. And then they ran away.

It was all a bit bizarre. Cocks flying in the air and cocks running for their lives.

But it was all good fun - despite Ellis Harrison getting his marching orders from referee McCartney late in the second half - and we stormed away as 1-0 winners with the firm and true belief that something very special was going to happen during the second leg at home. And we weren't disappointed with what was to take place four days later…

It's that feeling you get and you just know it's true and you can't explain why you know - you just do.

I had that feeling on the 3rd of May. I just knew we were going to be okay. I felt calm about what was coming and I knew I wasn't the only one.

Don't get me wrong - I was confident we'd take care of business at home in the second leg - but I felt something different regarding the final itself at Wembley.

I knew it was wrong to be assuming we'd get the right result for the second time against FGR in four days because - all joking aside - they're a good, hard team and they should never be underestimated. And their striker - Jon Parkin - he's dangerous. All jokes aside - that guy is the biggest and hardest goal scorer I've ever seen. If he gets hold of the ball at his feet anywhere near the eighteen yard box - you've got a big problem. And they don't come bigger than Parkin.

Our lads did themselves proud down there in the Conference. They had a shaky start and that was to be expected. It's always the same when you move up to or drop into a different league. But non-league football is tough. Our players got knocked around a lot and it took them a while to steady themselves. But they did. And that's testament to them coming together as a team with new blood in Matty Taylor, Daniel Leadbitter and Stuart Sinclair among others who bolstered the side which also saw Ellis Harrison shine despite doing is best to emulate his opposition at the *New Lawn* by 'thumping' their goalkeeper.

They were impressive. Not all the time. But they were when they had control of the game and played football on the floor instead of in the air. You can't compete with monsters when they're flying in the sky. But you can run rings around them once you chop off their wings and play the ball on the ground.

And I felt grounded before that second leg match at the Memorial Stadium as we milled around behind the Blackthorn End and enjoyed a drink before queuing to go in and grab our spot before we lost it to someone else in yet another sell-out crowd of just under eleven thousand.

Have you ever noticed how some supporters stand at - or on - the same spot for every home match? It's incredible. I used to have a chuckle when I started going to *The Mem* - to see grownups get upset if another supporter stood on their spot. And I'm talking about a specific spot on a concrete step! Not an area of a few feet square. I'm referring to exact pinpoint locations no bigger than the diameter of a football. I used to find it a bit silly to begin with. But not now. Stay away from my spot. Don't even think about it!

So we were standing in the queue and it looked like it was going to take a while - so I asked Helen and the others to look after my spot in the queue - which is a different spot to my spot in the stand - and went for a look around in the club shop. And that's when I saw it. It was hanging on the rack and it was blue and it was white and it was quarters - and it was my size!

Final match of the season at the Memorial Stadium and I land my first Bristol Rovers home jersey. Lush! And so I was a very happy boy when I emerged from the shop and walked towards our gang in the queue and they all smiled and gave a wee cheer as they saw me in my new colours. And it felt good. It felt the same as when I was a wee boy on Christmas morning in 1975 when I unwrapped what Santa had left me and saw the Scotland jersey. My first football colours. And the feeling of immense pride I had in that festive moment was exactly the same in that moment at the Memorial Stadium when we were anticipating our own festivities and all that stood in our way was an angry side from the *Shire* of Nailsworth.

I know it may sound a bit childish. I'm forty-seven now. But that's how I truly felt when I finally got hold of my first home jersey. It meant so much for me to get it after falling in love with the club at Dover and awakening to the truth that I was a *Gashead* too.

The colours are special to me. They represent new loves in my life after a long time in my own personal darkness. And I'm sure other *Gasheads* feel proud to wear their colours too for their own colourful reasons.

There was an explosion of noise when both teams emerged from the tunnel and I'm quietly confident it was our explosion - not their fans'. But that eruption of sound was nothing compared to the joyous bedlam which ensued thanks to the man who is '*one of our own..*'.

Chris Lines is a Bristol lad and he came up through the ranks at the club to feature in his first team debut at the age of twenty in a 2-1 win against Chester City in January 2006.

The midfielder was to make one hundred and sixty eight first team appearances for Rovers before a £50,000 move to Sheffield Wednesday in August 2011. And he was to play a key role in guiding them to clinch promotion to the Championship at the end of the 2011/2012 season.

Milton Keynes and Port Vale were to follow for Lines and as a true *Son of Irene* - he was to return to Filton Avenue just eight weeks before Matty Taylor's low cross into the eighteen yard box was afforded the perfect dummy by Big Bliss which allowed Chris Lines to thunder the ball in from nine yards and then race triumphantly into the orgy of sound and arms and joy of a sea of blue and white.

Eleven thousand voices filled the air on that sunny Sunday afternoon in the 24th minute of the game and a quarters-chorus of, *"He's one of our own. He's one of our own. Chrissy lines. He's one of our own!"* shot up into the blue and white sky and drifted above rooftops and across the streets and alleyways which surround and meander around and near the home of *The Gas.* And this sound in song was sung over and over again to our anthem of *'Goodnight Irene'* and *"Wemberly. Wemberly. We're the famous Bristol Rovers and we're going to Wemberley. Wemberley. Wemberley......"*

But on-form Matty Taylor wasn't convinced. He decided to be safe in the 88th minute and fired in a close range effort to guarantee our place in the Promotion Final. He really had to make sure he was going to Wembley. He'd arranged a date with some silverware.

And that was that. It was the third day of May and it was exactly one year after the Memorial Stadium was filled with tears of anguish and misery and anger at being relegated. Now this.

Scenes of tears but tears of joy. We'd fought our way back. We were sent down to a place where we found unity again. We were sent down to a place where we once again found our passion which was born from a history which surrounded us as we hugged and kissed and laughed and punched our fists in the air.

Our passion from our history was within and around the alleyways and streets which weave the stories and dreams and aspirations and disasters which have befallen us since our time began in 1883. And they still echo close to our hearts. They may have been quiet for a while. But they were never silent. Just quiet. But like a beauty in sleep - we kissed her close - our history true - and she awakened to take us to that hallowed place we know as Wembley.

"I was looking down to my right to see Lee Mansell being swamped by his Bristol Rovers team mates just seconds after his penalty hit the back of the net to return us to the Football League. My relief was immense. I turned to see my girl. She was in floods of tears. And the memory of her tearful joy from somewhere deep and true within her - will be one of the most endearing memories I'll ever have."

Those words are my one true memory of our Wembley Promotion Final. There are many others. But seeing Helen in floods of tears in genuine relief and happiness - after Lee Mansell netted our winning penalty - is one of the most endearing memories I'll ever have.

No more words are needed from me. Her tears said it all. We'd fought our way back to Football League Two. And we did it the hard way - *The Gas* way...

Call us *Ragbag* if you must. Call us *Tinpot* - we don't care. We've got fight and heart and passion for our club. And we stay 'til the end. Always the end...

Forty seven thousand supporters from both sides travelled to Wembley to watch the Promotion Final on that day - a day which saw us emerge winners over Grimsby Town who gave us a hard game - a game which saw me shaking uncontrollably with nerves for the duration of the match.

They took the lead within minutes of the final starting - but Ellis Harrison settled some nerves with the equaliser which took the game to extra time and penalities.

Our very own Chris Lines buried our first penalty. Mansell our fifth. And so we emerged victorious 5-3 winners after penalties and the Grimsby drum was silenced.

Scenes of elation were to ensue as Darrell Clarke sprinted towards the sea of blue and white - arms open wide – across the hallowed turf to receive our rapturous embrace as *Goodnight Irene* filled the home of English football. And it was witnessed all over the country too by television viewers who'd watched the match at home.

Social media was filled with congratulations from supporters from all over the United Kingdom. The nods of approval weren't just coming from fans - they were coming from true fans who understand what it feels like to love a club. And I'm quietly confident there were many tears from viewers far and wide as they watched our gaffer race towards us in the stands.

It was an incredible moment in time. It was the stuff dreams are made of as we all stood together - Helen, Simon, Claire, Dan and me. And we were also joined by Helen's daughter, Beth.

Beth's seen her own fair share of *Gas* highs and lows in her own twenty one years of following the club. She was at Wembley in May 2007 to watch Rovers clinch the League Two play-off final under Paul Trollope in a game which will always be remembered by *Gasheads* for Sammy Igoe's full-length-of-the-pitch run to score Rovers' third in the 3-1 win over Shrewsbury Town. So when we reach THIS season's Promotion Final - Beth's coming with us again whether she likes it or not!

Beth's best friend Sarah was with us too. And there was also someone else. He'd wanted to come along because - even though he's *one of them* - he wanted to be there because he wanted Rovers to win for Helen. She means that much to him.

But I think he's a *closet Gashead* and it's only a question of time because he was celebrating with the rest of us as we stayed and watched our lads celebrate on the pitch - surrounded by a mass of blue and white in song – and he also applauded as our captain Mark McChrystal hoisted the silverware which announced our right to return - before the cup made its way down from the presentation area and down the Wembley steps and into the Bristol Rovers dressing room where its date with Matty Taylor had been arranged. *Plenty of Fish* has a lot to answer for…

There weren't many fishermen remaining in the stadium by this point. Most of the Mariners had all but departed and it was tough to watch those who'd remained.

I couldn't empathise and I was grateful not to have to. They just stood in miserable, dazed silence with heads in hands and tears in eyes. The thought of a long coach ride back to Bristol if we'd lost would have been too much for me and the rest of us. So I was glad it was them and not us.

The Grimsby supporters did their side proud and they sang throughout the game and it was a game which was close - too close for my liking. But the clash between Bristol Rovers and Grimsby was to continue in a much different guise…

A certain newspaper editor with a certain Grimsby newspaper had expressed her discontent at something our gaffer had said whilst out celebrating with his team prior to the final. Darrel Clarke was heard to say, *"We're going up!"* whilst enjoying a quiet glass of wine with his squad. And the editor didn't like it. She said he was 'gloating' and she was very unhappy.

A small furore then ensued in the build up to the final. But this was quickly resolved when we did indeed win promotion and a short while afterwards - whilst enjoying another small glass of wine with his team before - our manager was heard to whisper the words which finally put a stop to all the fuss, *"Print that bastard!"*

It was the perfect full stop to the season!

11 IT'S IN THE CUP

Bristol Rovers v Wycombe Wanderers
Memorial Stadium, 1ˢᵗ December 2015
7.45pm kick-off

Your face is itchy as you look to the black sky above the away
supporters' unsheltered section at your home ground and you're
grateful it's exposed to the elements from all directions and you
know your thoughts may sound harsh but you also know they're
perfectly justified because it wasn't really that long ago that your
team were robbed of a win and three points by this lot's side
when you were playing them away and their safety official called
for the game to be abandoned because he thought the
Gasheads' stand was in imminent danger from God.

Your team were 3-1 up against Wycombe Wanderers and it was
highly unlikely the home side could clinch the two or three goals
required to save face from a home thumping and also save face
from supporting a side nicknamed *The Chairboys* - apt in the
irony that they won't be able to sit down for the next few hours
and they'll find it all a bit confusing when proceedings

commence and they hear our chant of *"Sit down shut up"* because there's only cold emptiness in the away end and it's a bit like the amount of hope which now remains at Yeovil Town concerning avoiding relegation.

You continue to scratch your face as you slip your fifty-fifty-half-time-draw tickets into your back pocket and it's as you do this you see the lead singer of *The Cure* standing over to your right - wearing the colours of the *Blue Army* - and you think to yourself, *"Feck me - Robert Smith hasn't aged a bit!"*

But then you realise it's just the re-emergence of eighties fashion as skinny legs in skinny jeans support big jackets and bigger hair and you chuckle as you remember you used to look and dress like that too - back in the day – and you also remember how you used to be devastating on the dancefloor to the *rockin'* tunes of *The Clash* and *New Order* and *The Smiths* as you gyrated your way around the girls beneath the flashing lights whilst swigging on a bottle of beer, looking cool as feck - but never quite sure why you always went home alone?

But now you know. You now know because age has blessed you with wisdom and that wisdom informs you that you looked like a hairy, dancing knob in jeans that were so tight you had to stitch yourself into them. So you were a knob who could sew. But you were indeed 'devastating' because your 'unique' fashion look devastated any chances you had of being invited for a *'fumble'*…

So you know it's true what they say when they say, *"What goes around comes around!"* And then your heart chuckles as you wonder if the same might happen in football with the return of players with perms and moustaches and tiny tight shorts - so tight and tiny that sister *Gasheads* (and some brothers) will gaze in awe at players they've never gazed in awe at before. And the *'Horfield Hottie Top Ten'* would be hurriedly rearranged as proof that *'size does matter'* when you see the player with the biggest bulge enter the number one spot!

And it's with that thought of massive bellends that you once again look over to the away enclosure where you see them shine beneath the floodlight of *'guilty'* and ponder whether the Wycombe safety official at that game - not that long ago - did actually know that an airstrike from Heaven was about to transform *Gasheads* into gas - because if he did - then that would make him a prophet - not a safety officer.

But you know that just doesn't make sense because why on earth would someone with the ability to transcend space and time to jump into the future to see up-and-coming events support Wycombe Wanderers? So you realise that's all the evidence you need to dispel his past claims of the imminent twenty billion volt threat. And that wouldn't happen anyway - because *Gasheads* are *'the chosen ones'*!

So you reach the conclusion the wannabe seer from Wycombe was just being a bit of a knob who indulged in his own pity party and made the whole thing up about being able to see into the future and what was about to befall the *Blue Army*. And you know that means he was tempting fate and Karma because Karma sees and hears everything from the present and past and then makes a divine decision on what the future holds for those who mess with her. So you're still clawing at your face when you look to the night sky and wonder if she'll make her presence known to the hundreds of away supporters in the shape of a vapourising bolt from Celeste? But you're also aware that being charged a lot isn't something new to Wycombe Wanderers' supporters!

You're still scratching your face well into the first half of your team's home match against the boys who like chairs who do chairs like they're girls and you're wondering if Blur will ever make an album to beat that one and you're hoping to hell your lads can beat a side supported by deck chair lovers (not because

they have a subjecting appreciation for stripy upholstery)
because this home win is crucial following your sides late, late
horror show when you stood in a puddle in a place called *The
Shed* to see a tool score the equaliser which robbed you and your
team and your fellow *Gasheads* of a glorious three points after
The Pirate King - Stu Sinclair - delivered a masterclass lesson to
the footballing world on what to do with a ball just outside the
eighteen yard box and it was his vision of hairy-perfection
which inspired you to try and grow a beard to pay homage to
your *Pirate King* - but now three days of not shaving sees you
feel like something horrible and itchy has attacked your face and
you hope it's the hair growth and not some kind of pestilence -
because you had to walk through Bedminster yesterday.

So the half time whistle blows and it's no score and that horrible
feeling befalls you from above and and below and all around
you as you're now you're worried because you had a good
feeling about this game and now you don't - so you dip into
your back pocket to find some hope that you've clinched the
fifty-fifty draw and if you have - then you can afford to see a
dermatologist for some professional advice on whether or not
your face-on-fire is courtesy of hair? And if he says no, then
you'll need to ask him if *The Plague* still exists within the vicinity
of Ashton Gate? And your concerns are real because they all
look as if *The Plague* still exists within the vicinity of Ashton
Gate.

So it's with pestilence at the forefront of your mind that you
hear an almighty scream and your first thought is *Captain Gas*.
And the reason why your club's giant Pirate mascot comes to
the forefront of your mind in a flash is because you've had an
uncomfortable feeling about him for a while and it all began a
few weeks ago when you had a *'selfie'* taken with him and as you
held him close - you had a horrible feeling he's all just a front
and something sinister lurks beneath.

You remember how you put it down to just being a bit paranoid and how that always tends to happen when you hug strange men in big costumes - but there was definitely something 'untoward' going on beneath the foam and he wasn't speaking and there was no smile and he didn't say goodbye - so you know it's possible he's on the run and being a mascot is the perfect hiding place for a serial killer on the loose. It's more than the perfect disguise. It's genius.

So you hear the screaming during the interval and it's really loud and that's because it's coming from someone really close - but you can't see *Captain Gas* anywhere. So your weeks-long theory of your mighty mascot being a monster within a pirate is quickly dispelled and that's a pity - because with the right support and intelligence gathering and guidance - you could have sent him to sort out *'them down the road'* after turning him into BRFC's very own *Dexter*!

You see your friend Claire jumping up and down and she's screaming and she's waving her hands in the air and you know you're not the reason because your hands are in your pockets - but you find out she's won the second place fifty-fifty prize of one hundred pounds and you're delighted for her as she heads to collect her winnings with Helen and you're hoping Helen hasn't forgotten her pickpocket skills which she acquired in her childhood days from a neighbour who was a City fan.

And so Claire is flush - but not as flush as your screaming itching face as the game restarts and it's on the hour mark when perfection takes place from a free-kick and the man who had the date with some silver at Wembley emerges from a beautifully worked set-piece with Lee Mansell and thunders a right-footed shot into the top right hand corner from nineteen yards out and the screaming begins again and it's not just Claire - it's every other *Gashead* in the ground and it's nothing less than an eruption of sound as Matty Taylor turns to the west stand and receives the adulation he deserves for such a clinical finish and it's all just perfect.

But he isn't finished yet because just moments later it's a free kick in almost the same spot and it's quick thinking by Stuart Sinclair to take the free kick quickly and Taylor's there yet again and he strikes again and it's two goals in two minutes and it's a second explosion of noise from over six thousand jubilant voices in blue and white and Taylor races to the front of the Blackthorn End and into the arms of rapture as the sound of, *"His cock's in the Cup. His cock's in the Cup. Matty Taylor. His cock's in the Cup"* swirls around *The Mem*!

You're jumping up and down and you're so happy you think you might wee yourself and you wonder if anyone will notice as the chorus in celebration changes from one song to another and it's perfect because it's Karma and she has indeed returned - but not quite the way you thought she would - because Karma has returned to the tune of *'Chirpy Chirpy Cheep Cheep'* as the blue and white choir bellow out, *"Where's your lightning gone - where's your lightning gone? Where's your lightning gone - where's your lightning gone?"* to the Wycombe supporters as you laugh to the black night sky and give elated thanks to the Heavens above and the truth of *'what comes around goes around...'*

The Blackthorn End is jumping and you're jumping too as a mass of hands reach for the stars to bestow your own star - who dates Cups - with fervent appraisal and once again you hear the sounds echo around *The Mem* - the sound of the song conceived at home against Carlisle, *"We're winning at home. We're winning at home. How shit must you be? We're winning at home!"* and you know in your heart amid the sound of song that this is what it's all about in being a *Gashead* - the highs and the lows and this is a high you'll always remember. But your striker isn't done...

You watch in awe as *Mighty Matty* quite literally runs rings around their hapless keeper - Matt Ingram - and nets his third.

Three goals in twelve minutes. And it's just a bit special because Taylor clinches three in twelve in our third home win of the season and if you divide twelve by three you get four and there's an *Apocalypse* which has befallen the away end as the Wycombe supporters are standing looking more hapless than their keeper and they're just waiting for the *Four Horsemen* to arrive! And they do. And one of them is called Matty. And he's riding Silver!

And so you skip away from the Memorial Stadium with your head held high as you hold her hand as you leave the ground and turn left onto Filton Avenue and then left again onto Gloucester Road and you're hoping the night is filled with headlights from buses and cars as they spotlight your joy as you stride triumphant and smile at faces unseen within the glare of the traffic and you're hesitant to turn left again onto Strathmore Road because you want your moment in the headlights beneath the starlight to announce to the world that you're a *Gashead* and that feels incredible on this night of three in twelve on the first day of December and it's the best start to the festive season you could possibly hope for...

And with that - you do turn and enter the darkness of a street lit up with the sounds of fans strolling homewards amid the soft echo of *Goodnight Irene*...

12 THE FORTRESS

Sometimes in life things happen when you don't expect them to happen...

I was feeling not worthy and the feeling seeped in just after I arrived on a sloping parking lot not far from Bath city centre on a beautiful, sunny winter's morning - just three days after the three which Taylor delivered to stun the visiting Wycombe side in a twelve minute spell which left us all spellbound and the Memorial Stadium bouncing!

It was actually on that night - whilst standing in the Blackthorn end scratching my face - that I decided I'd construct the final chapters of this book at the place where the final words should really be found - Twerton Park aka *'Fortess Twerton'*.

It felt right for me to find these words there. I know Eastville was our spiritual home and no longer exists. But it felt right for me to search for the final words at the ground we once shared with Bath City FC all those years ago, when we had nowhere else to go. They took us in. And it was within their welcome embrace that a time of football magic happened for our club...

So many stories I've heard from fellow *Gasheads* since I fell in love with the club - stories from so many memories shared by wonderful people who saw and lived and breathed incredible scenes on the pitch as they followed Bristol Rovers FC - from the beginnings of their own personal journeys in blue and white until right here and right now as I sit in my car writing these words. And it was here in this special place - twenty five years ago - that a lesson was taught as *Faithful and True* triumphed over our rivals - Bristol City.

The 2nd of May 1990 is the day in our club's history which will forever be remembered by *Gasheads* following that 3-0 thumping of *'them down the road'* which I wrote about earlier in this book. And it's arguably the *Day of all Days* for all supporters of the *Blue Army*.

I now know that to be true. But I only know that now. I'd heard from so many of you just how important that day was for all of you - but then I found myself sitting in the car park – not far from where it all happened and the enormity of it all hit me.

I genuinely didn't feel worthy enough to walk into such a special place. And it's a place where I'm told - if we went down one-nil while Gerry Francis was our gaffer - it meant we'd more than likely end up winning the game.

You've all shared with me of how we - Bristol Rovers - didn't have much back then. I suppose the same could said for now too. We may not have had a lot of cash to throw around in 1990 – but I've been told we had something which was more valuable than money and it did earn us success. We had a proper team under Francis. A team which played for the jersey. And I feel that now - in its past truth - as I sit in my car and write these words just a few yards away from where the events of that day took place.

We weren't flash like the others. We still aren't. And we weren't on that day twenty five years ago when we silenced those who mocked us with words like *'Tinpot'* and *'Ragbag'*.

To those who still use those words to describe us, I say this - call us *'Tin Pot'* - if you must. Call us *'Ragbag'* - we don't care. We don't care because what we care about is our history true - from where in time we come from.

Ours is a history with a true beginning. Our is a history which began one hundred and thirty two years ago. And it's founded in strength of heart with passion and fight. And that heart and passion and fight remains. We've proved that under Darrell Clarke.

'Tin Pot' and *'Ragbag'*? Perhaps. But we have a wealth that you will never have. We have a solidarity in unity. And that's priceless.

They came to our borrowed home on the 2nd of May 1990 and we put them in their place. Second. And that's what a club with a genuine history can do...

And so it was with all of your memories - so kindly shared - and video footage watched over and over again, that I emerged from my car to enter the stadium where that incredible result took place - courtesy of Gerry Francis and his lads.

Looking across my left shoulder - I saw the rear of the green stands and my stomach tightened with nerves. I hadn't expected this feeling to happen. The journey from Bristol to Bath had been filled with so many memories...

13 MEMORIES OF MAY

I'd been okay earlier in the car as I departed Kingswood and then dropped Helen's youngest daughter Meg at college - to then drive the Keynsham Bypass towards Bath.

The journey didn't take that long but all the while I was thinking about the supporters we have and the players we have and the manager we have and the club we all love. My thoughts turned to Darrell Clarke and how he stood in tears at the end of last season after we were relegated and how one supporter tried to console him on the pitch at *The Mem*. One of our own looking out for one of our own - because as football supporters we all want the same thing and that wanting is born from a history from flesh and blood and nurtured within the brick and plaster of the homes on the streets and alleyways which embrace and meander around the club we all love. That wanting cements our unity - because we are our club.

I then remembered how we all stood by our team and supported them throughout our Conference campaign and how our *Blue Army* smashed away supporter attendance records all over the country and how we believed in our hearts that if our lads had to play on bomb crater surfaces - then we'd be there with them and cheer them on as they battled on bomb crater surfaces - because that's what we do for our own.

The tears are welling up right now as I write these words - because all of this really means something to me and I'm sure Bristol Rovers really means something to you too as you read these words.

I don't mind the tears. I don't mind because it means I'm a proper *Gashead*. I feel for my club - from so very deep within me.

We went through so many highs and so many lows. Being a supporter of our club is a bit like being bipolar. But you wouldn't want it any other way - because a true fan is one who feels hurt when your side loses and elation when they win.

And it was on a high that I steered the car along the Keynsham Bypass and then into Bath Road when I remembered how angry our supporters were when we were sent down on that day last year - and how I truly believe that those who own football clubs have a duty of care to the club. And because the supporters and their history are the club - then those who own have a duty to those who follow to never allow that to ever happen again. A football club isn't a football club without supporters.

Generations of the blue and white army have followed Bristol Rovers since the very beginning. Hearts in faith in the here and now born from those who witnessed the dawn of the club. Our family club has a duty to always do the best it can for its family.

But we came back from the abyss. We went there with our lads and we returned with our lads. And it was one helluva journey.

The vision of our gaffer sprinting across the hallowed turf at Wembley - after Mansell's penalty clinched promotion - epitomised the relief and elation and the pride of us all.

It was as I was nearing the railway archway on Lower Bristol Road - about to turn right into Connection Road - that my thoughts turned to our squad and what they've achieved and continue to achieve and do their very best to achieve. I'm truly proud of each and every one of them.

We currently sit 10th in League Two - a league from which we were sent down not that long ago into a non-league darkness from which many will never be able to escape. And for them - that will be there unfortunate destiny.

It's fair to say we should never have ended up down there. Yes, Wembley was a celebration - but it was also a wake-up call from my own point of view. And as much as it was an exciting and unforgettable season – I'd prefer not to do it again.

It doesn't have to be our destiny. I don't feel it will be. But I do feel there's a change coming and it'll be for the better. A freshness for our club. It's as if something awaits for us - something we deserve - and it's been waiting a long time. And I base that feeling on the events of the past two seasons. It's as if we had to be humbled to become stronger for the next stage in our club's history. We had to be broken to be built again. To be built for a new challenge. I'm not a betting man. I've indulged in enough vices during my time. But I'd put money on us making the play-offs and causing a storm. And it wouldn't surprise me if we go up again at the end of this season

I feel for them - the other clubs struggling in the lower leagues. And that feeling was with me as I pulled into the car park at Bath City FC and then felt unworthy to enter. But I did. And I entered via the Randall's clubhouse.

I wasn't expecting anything different to the welcome I received.

It was a warm welcome as I was ushered through the bar and into a whitewashed brick tunnel were I was introduced to two members of the club's ground staff who have nothing less than fond memories of Bristol Rovers' time at Twerton.

They told me how the Popular Stand was were the *Gasheads* liked to stand and watch the games and how our supporters behaved: *"We never had any trouble with the Gasheads!"* And they also told me how they benefitted from us ground sharing with them - following the fire at Eastville.

It seems our presence at Twerton afforded them the finances to refurbish certain parts of their ground - including the erection of a new stand. And what made me smile within was when they told me what they call their new stand, *"We refer to it as our family stand!"*

And with that - I was informed I could go wherever I wanted to go and take pictures and write wherever I wanted to write. The book was about being a *Gashead* with Bristol Rovers - a family club. And they were more than okay with me being there. That's what you'd expect from lower league sides.

They're real. And I've had the good fortune to experience that many times - an experience which began all those years ago when I was a young producer producing *Football First* with Scottish Television. And that openness was what drew me to Bristol Rovers in the first place…

So as I climbed the stone steps - I remembered Helen telling me about how they used to play Del Shannon's *Runaway* before every Rovers home game at *Fortress Twerton*. And so I had the song in my head as I reached the top of the steps and saw the Popular Stand straight ahead of me. I then looked to my right and saw the dugouts. And then I became emotional.

It just hit me as I remembered the jubilant scenes of *Gasheads* celebrating in song to the sound of, *"Will you ever beat the Gas?"* And I remembered how Joe had to suffer at the hands of his own fans. But my depth of feeling had nothing to do with them. It was as if part of me had connected to that that time and I was filled with pride - the way you all were on that day. And I just stood on one spot and gazed around me and I didn't want to leave.

Part of me told me I didn't deserve to feel this way because I'm not from Bristol. But another part of me reminded me that it was Bristol that gave me a second chance with a new life and new loves and within that second chance I'd found Bristol Rovers. And then I felt okay - because Bristol will now be forever my home and *The Gas* forever my club.

So I just took a deep breath and exhaled and looked over to the goalposts where Devon White and Ian Holloway scored two of our three goals that day - and I felt an incredible sense of belonging. And being at Twerton and feeling so proud will be a feeling within a memory which I will remember 'til my end of days.

I really didn't want to leave. So I started to write and what you're reading now include words assembled at Twerton.

So I was standing next to the dugouts - when a man wandered over to me. I explained about the book and he was fine with me being at the ground. He was casually dressed and he was carrying a screwdriver. He introduced himself as one of the Bath City directors - Phil Weaver - and he's a lovely bloke.

Phil pointed to the blue seats above us in the main stand and told me they'd acquired a lot of them from Manchester City following the demolition of Maine Road. The stand also has seats from Leicester City's Filbert Street and Chesterfield FC's old Recreation Ground.

We chatted a bit more and then he had to excuse himself because he had to fix one of the floodlights - hence the screwdriver! Now that's real football for you!

Sometimes things happen in life when you don't expect them too...

I thought my welling of tears had gone for good as I'd found my worthiness to stand and look at the hallowed spot where *Bruno* and *Ollie* had silenced City - but I was wrong!

Standing in front of the dugouts - I positioned myself so that the goal mouth where they scored could be seen over my shoulder. I then took a selfie and posted it on the BRFC Facebook page. And the response from *Gasheads* from far and wide blew me away!

The posts in the thread were incredible. Supporters reminiscing about that day on the 2nd of May 1990 and how special Twerton was and still is to them. True fans sharing their own fond memories of that stunning result in such a special place - a place owned by a club which gave us a home when we had no home.

I knew the final chapter of this book had to be written at Twerton. But what I didn't know before arriving at the Bath ground was that some of the memories shared by *Gasheads* on Facebook would also feature within the final pages.

Some things happen in life when you don't expect them to.

The following are courtesy of Gasheads who have given me permission to use their words. And I've made an editorial decision to include all words.

It is what it is! It's being a football fan!

UTG RTID!

'I was there with my dad and best friend. Since my days of following The Gas from Eastville as a kid through promotions and famous cup wins at The Mem and Wembley - nothing will ever be better that night.' **Mark Galsworthy**

'They (Bath City FC) are a good club. They allowed us to use their facilities for next to nothing in the summer when we hosted a charity football match at the ground. They helped us raise about £1,600 for CLIC Sargent. And my profile picture was taken with the dugouts at Twerton just behind the camera'. **Dave Southgate**

'Went to every game at Twerton. We played some big teams like Liverpool, Aston Villa and Man City. Not many teams liked playing at '*Fortess Twerton*'. Wimbledon played a testimonial game for Jack Pitt, bringing the FA cup with them. Who remembers the streaker during the Liverpool game? He jumped into the crowd asking if anyone had spare trousers? Loved the Twerton days. Felt more like home than *The Mem*.' **Paula Marie Gadsby**

'Phoned from Australia to get the result at The Beeches in Broomhill. It was always full of *shitheads*. They weren't happy about the result. I went out after work in Coogee beach and got roaring drunk with two other Gasheads. Whoop! Whoop! Whoop!' **Martyn Hillier**

'That was a brilliant night John. The *shitheads* were spitting on their manager Joe Jordan - throwing their toys out their prams. And the advertising hoardings. We all laughed from *The Shed* end. What a night. I'll never forget it!' Jeff Dickens

'Fortress Twerton. Oh Happy Days!' **Lesley Allen**

'What a night that was. I was there with my dad. I remember Joe Jordan having to go over and placate the 'Teds' who were ripping up advertising boards. We could here *Goodnight Irene* clear as day as we were walking back to the car afterwards. We made the trip to Blackpool after that too. Great times to be a *Gashead*!' **Kevin Adderley**

'You had to park your car on a demolished building site and walk over a bridge to walk up to the ground pre H&S. Just a great buzz walking up through the area, away teams must of thought – this IS League standard. I'm glad you can appreciate that feeling, John. We were like Wimbledon in reverse!' **Alan Long**

'Had an amazing season there when I fecked my back up playing footy. I saw nearly every home game in the promotion year. I also remember the carnage when we sent WBA down. That was a crazy day.' **Simon Fox**

'What a night that was! Pure heaven! I was stood near the tea shack on the main stand side along with my two sons, Simon and Tim and Steve Yates' Dad. Memories!' **Bob Bruton**

'Great post and amazing memories from the place I fell in love with Rovers. I remember the noise and the feet stamping on the wooden terrace and the three bus journey to get there and the best bit was the Twerton chippy!!!!' **James Shorney**

'One of the best nights of my life. Getting promoted and smashing the shit! Happy Days!' **David Holmes**

'A wonderful evening, weather was kind and people were climbing up the floodlights to get a better view. Took my son, Paul, into Leigh Delamare on the way back up the M4 and that was the best fish and chips I've ever tasted in my life!!' **David Colley**

'Such happy memories of the place where I fell in love with football and with Rovers. Me, my dad Jim and my sister Corinne used to get there really early on a Saturday so we could get a spot by the wall at the front of the Popular side (so we could see!) and then fill our time before kick-off calling the players who were warming up over to sign our evil post-match pull outs and pose for photos. They were all brilliant. Poor Marcus Stewart (who I was ever so slightly in love with as a teenager) must have signed his name for me dozens of times over the years!!' **Kim Price**

'Simply the best! And don't forget when we went there we were down and out only to rise again under Gerry. SO many memories from those days - from the 'down' days with 3,000 fans to the *'Gerry and The Dreammakers'* days with nigh on 10,000 there. When Bruno scored 1st goal on 2nd of May I celebrated so much I ruptured ligaments in my ankle. I'd been to 35 games that season so stayed until the end (thank god!) and was carried out on mate's shoulder at end of game. A load of Ted morons came charging up one of the entrances and I've never hopped so fast in my life! I've still got the manky old plaster cast signed by all the championship winning team! It's in the loft as my wife will not allow it in the house. She just doesn't understand!' **Nick Nasse**

'I was there. Best football night ever!' **Graham Heale**

'I went down to most matches that season. It was indeed a pleasure to see the thumping we gave them from over the river. In fact, there was an even better thumping when Big Mal arrived for the last matches of his illustrious career and we walloped them 4-0. All goals were spectacular as well. Looked brilliant on TV. Even better to be there. I was there and watched 43 out of 46 games that season. Best time of my life bar my wedding day.' **Bobby Charlton**

'Yep I was there with my father. God bless him.' **John Harris**

'I hate Bath with all its Grade 3 listed bollocks. But the working class area of Twerton treated us *Gas* absolutely brilliantly. If it wasn't for that great little club helping us out we could have gone under. And don't forget we may have given them some cash(not much) but they lost support for their own club as some locals drifted over to us. We used to stop off at the Crown in Kelston on our way over and the locals would visibly brace themselves as we walked in. So may happy memories. Thanks for a great article!' **Daniel Hill**

'Absolutely fantastic times filled with great memories & when things could have been all so different as a club - we all pulled together and achieved great things and now we have wonderful memories. Thank you *Gasheads* for all the support you gave us!' **Christian Mcclean (former Bristol Rovers player)**

'Don't think anyone has mentioned this yet - the famous song of the Popular Side. It was the season after 1990 promotion and it was a version of the hymn, repeated: *"All things bright and beautiful, All creatures great and small. Rovers won the Championship. And City won f*** all ... AGAIN!"* **Anonymous**

'I broke my ankle at a Barnet game at the Bath End. I was a bit enthusiastically drunk at Twerton. It was just before half time when we scored our third and I knew I'd broken it when I was celebrating.

But I refused to go to hospital until we finished scoring. We won 6-1 I think. I had to be stretchered off with fifteen minutes to go. It hurt so much. I said hello to the then manager of Barnet - Ray Clemence as I passed him on the stretcher. I'll never forget that! I had a tennis ball lump on my ankle. Love Rovers so much it hurt! My name is Bobby Charlton for real! **Bobby Charlton**

'Famous FA Cup game against Liverpool in 1992. It ended a 1-1 draw with Carl Saunders scoring past a certain Bruce Grobbelaar. Happy memories!' **Simon Parkin-Everson**

'The best games I ever saw were at Twerton watching Rovers from the Popular side. Some great Bristol Derby matches. Watching Liverpool and Manchester City was great - but nothing will beat the 3-0 win over Bristol City to not only win the Derby but win the league. It was brilliant. Good memories of Devon White being marked by about 4 defenders on a corner and he would still win the header. He never looked a natural footballer but was quality at scoring goals. Billy Ocean was also a great scorer for the gas. And Mehew scored plenty from midfield. The list goes on and on.... Best days at Twerton!' **Sean Stone**

'The Liverpool FA Cup tie was a highlight - holding them to a draw watched by a record crowd at Twerton.' **Mike Jay**

14 GASHEAD

Twerton Park
Bath, 4ᵗʰ December 2015
12.30pm

I'm sitting at Twerton and my phone alerts to your posts on the thread are still coming in...

I'm sitting above the dugouts in the main stand and I'm sure the black seat on which I sit comes from Chesterfield FC's old ground.

And I'm wondering how many supporters in Derbyshire sat in this same seat and endured the highs and lows of being true to their own team and how many of them looked up to the night sky in awe - with arms outstretched to try and touch the stars after one of their own stars wearing their own colours netted a stormer which saw their ground explode in sound of song?

We may belong to different tribes - but we're all part of the same family. Football supporters...

Upon the Chesterfield seat within the grounds of Bath City FC - I look over to my left and into the rays of the winter sunshine which cascade down from the blue sky and they produce an almost-dreamlike haze around the goalposts where Bruno and Ollie scored number two and number three. And as I sit in this empty special place - I close my eyes and imagine you all - thousands of Gasheads - with arms reaching upwards as the explosion of sound with elation thunders all around in a moment in time which will always be remembered and never be forgotten.

Call me *'Ragbag'* - if you must. Call me *'Tinpot'* - I don't care.

I know what it means to be without a home. I know what it means to be penniless and lost. And I know what it feels like to have someone to help me find hope...

Bath City FC helped Bristol Rovers FC when we had nowhere else to go. That's good enough for me. And so this place will always be special to me for two reasons - the result on the 2nd of May 1990 and the part Twerton played in our club's history.

I found hope in Bristol. Then I found love. And then within that love I found Bristol Rovers. And you can't put a price on that!

I'm now a grateful man. I have a new home with my new family. And I also have my *Gas* family. And I wish I could have been here with you on that day twenty five years ago. But being here right now - I can feel your memories resonate from that time and it feels as if you're all here with me right now. And it feels incredible.

That means I care about Bristol Rovers. That means I love the club. And that makes me smile - because that makes me a Gashead. And that makes me faithful and true.

UTG RTID

ABOUT THE AUTHOR

John Thomson is a freelance filmmaker who lives in Bristol.

He lives with his partner Helen and her daughters Beth and Meg. A Bristol City supporter also lives with them - however - he wishes to remain anonymous.

John is a producer, director and editor who makes a living making films of all kinds - from promos for businesses to documentaries.

His business Grateful Productions has been running for three years and is founded on his twelve years broadcasting experience with Scottish Television/STV Sport as a journalist/producer/director.

He is now a Gashead.

Printed in Great Britain
by Amazon.co.uk, Ltd.,
Marston Gate.